PÉTAIN

MILITARY PROFILES

SERIES EDITOR

Dennis E. Showalter, Ph.D.

Colorado College

*Instructive summaries for general and expert
readers alike, volumes in the Military Profiles
series are essential treatments of significant and
popular military figures drawn from world history,
ancient times through the present.*

PÉTAIN

Verdun to Vichy

Robert B. Bruce, Ph.D.

Potomac Books, Inc.
Washington, D.C.

Library of Congress Cataloging-in-Publication Data

Bruce, Robert B. (Robert Bowman), 1963-
  Pétain : Verdun to Vichy / by Robert B. Bruce.— 1st ed.
      p. cm. — (Potomac military profiles)
  Includes bibliographical references.
  ISBN 978-1-57488-598-9 (hardcover : alk. paper)
  ISBN 978-1-57488-757-0 (pbk. : alk. paper)
  1. Pétain, Philippe, 1856-1951. 2. Marshals—France—Biography. 3. France. Armée—Biography. 4. Heads of state—France—Biography. 5. France—History, Military—20th century. 6. France—Politics and government—20th century. I. Title.
  DC342.8.P4B84 2008
  944.081'6092—dc22

                                            2008003373

Printed in the United States of America on acid-free paper that meets the American National Standards Institute Z39-48 Standard.

Potomac Books, Inc.
22841 Quicksilver Drive
Dulles, Virginia 20166

First Edition

10 9 8 7 6 5 4 3 2 1

Contents

	List of Maps	vii
	Preface	ix
	Chronology	xi
Chapter 1	The Making of a Soldier, 1856–1914	1
Chapter 2	Heretic to Prophet: The 1914 and 1915 Campaigns	17
Chapter 3	The Victor of Verdun, 1916	33
Chapter 4	Commander in Chief of the French Army, 1917–1918	53
Chapter 5	Between World Wars, 1918–1939	71
Chapter 6	The Fall of France, Vichy, and Exile	89
	Notes	115
	Bibliographic Essay	119
	Index	123
	About the Author	125

Maps

Champagne Offensives, 1915   xiv
Battle of Verdun, 1916   xv
Western Front, ca. 1916   xvi

Preface

Few figures in modern French history are more controversial than Marshal Philippe Pétain. He rose from obscurity in 1914 to become a general and led the French army to victory in the bloody crucible of Verdun. Appointed commanding general of the French army in 1917, he rallied the French soldiers and led them to triumph in the Great War. His brilliant theories of firepower and deep empathy for his soldiers mark him as one of the greatest Allied generals of World War I. Yet today he is best remembered as the nearly senile octogenarian who was handed the reins of power in France in the midst of the disastrous 1940 campaign and sought an armistice with Hitler's Germany. Pétain's subsequent leadership of Vichy France from 1940 to 1944 marked his descent into collaboration with the Nazis and the destruction of all that he had stood for throughout his life. His postwar conviction for treason and lifetime exile to the Île d'Yeu marked an ignominious end to a once brilliant career.

This book is a military biography and as such covers Pétain's service in the Great War in detail but is far less focused on his political role as head of the collaborationist Vichy regime during World War II. My intent throughout the book has been to neither celebrate nor condemn Pétain. Rather I have tried to illuminate his military career, and by extension the French army he served in, and to show how and why he became one of the greatest French military commanders of the twentieth century. At the same time, the story of Pétain would be incomplete without some discussion of his role in Vichy. Therefore, I have eschewed the trend of his other military biographers and dealt with significant issues of 1940 to 1945, while still keeping the focus on military affairs.

By no means is this book, limited as it is in size and scope by the constraints of Potomac's Military Profiles series, meant to be a definitive work on Pétain. It is hoped, however, that it will provide an introduction to the man and his career and spark an interest in the reader to delve deeper into the issues it discusses.

I would like to thank Dennis Showalter, who first approached me with the idea of doing a military biography of Pétain, as well as Paul Merzlak, who first signed me to the contract. I would also like to extend a special thanks to Don Jacobs at Potomac Books, who demonstrated tremendous patience and understanding over the course of the writing of this book and continued to have faith in the project and encourage me throughout the final stages of its writing.

I want to extend a special thanks to my beloved wife Dr. Susannah U. Bruce, who is an accomplished Civil War historian and author in her own right, for always being there to listen. Over the course of the writing of this book and others, Susannah has heard more about the French army in the twentieth century than any Civil War scholar should rightfully have to tolerate. Finally I want to thank my three-year-old son, Robby, for reminding me when it was time to leave the wars behind and play, read stories, or simply dream together.

Chronology

1856	Henri Philippe Benoni Omer Pétain is born at Cauchy-à-la-Tour, France.
1877	Graduates from Saint-Cyr.
1878–1888	Serves with Chasseurs and Chasseurs Alpin's regiments.
1890	Graduates from the École de Guerre.
1893–1899	Serves on the staff of the commander of the military division of Paris.
1900	Is assigned as an instructor at École de Tir in Châlons.
1901–1911	Is appointed as an instructor in infantry tactics at École de Guerre.
1911	Is promoted to colonel and named commanding officer of the Thirty-third Infantry Regiment.
1913	Is named commanding officer of the Fourth Infantry Brigade, Second Infantry Division.
1914	The Great War begins in August, and Pétain is promoted to *général de brigade* and named commander of the Sixth Infantry Division. The Battle of the Marne begins in September. Pétain is promoted to *général de division* and then named commander of XXXIII Corps.
1915	The first Artois offensive ends in January, and the second Artois offensive commences in April and runs through May. Pétain is named commander of the French Second Army in June. The Champagne offensive runs through September and October.
1916	The Battle of Verdun begins in February, and Pétain is named commander of French forces at Verdun. In April

he is appointed commanding general of the Central Army Group. By July the Germans make their final attempt to capture Verdun. The French launch successful counteroffensives at Verdun in October and December.

1917   The Nivelle offensive begins in April and so do the French army mutinies. Pétain is named commanding general of the French Armies of the North and Northeast in May, and the French army mutinies end in July.

1918   The German offensives begin in March and rupture French lines at Chemin des Dames in May. The Second Battle of the Marne begins in July. General Allied offensives begin in September. The Great War ends in November. Pétain is named marshal of France in December.

1919   The Treaty of Versailles is signed in July.

1920   Pétain is named vice chair of the Supreme War Council and commander in chief in time of war. He marries Eugénie Hardon.

1922   The office of inspector general of the French army is added to Pétain's responsibilities.

1925   Is appointed commander of French forces in the Rif War.

1926   Franco-Spanish armies win the Rif War.

1930   Construction of the Maginot Line begins.

1931   Pétain is inducted into the Académie Française. He retires from his post of commander in chief of the French army. Heads the French delegation to the United States for the 150th anniversary of the Battle of Yorktown and is appointed inspector general of air defense.

1934   Is appointed minister of war.

1935   The Maginot Line is completed, and Pétain resigns from his post as minister of war.

1936   The German army moves into the Rhineland, and Belgium withdraws from its alliance with France.

1939   Pétain is appointed ambassador to Spain. World War II begins in September.

1940   The German offensive in the West begins in May, and Pétain is named vice premier. In June the Germans capture Paris, Pétain is named chief of state, and France signs an armistice with Germany. The British Royal Navy destroys the French fleet at Mers-el-Kébir in July, and *L'État Français* (Vichy France) is established. Pétain meets with Hitler at Montoire in October.

1942   In November Anglo-American and Free French forces invade Algeria and Morocco, and the German army invades and occupies Vichy France.

1943   Pétain approves the creation of the Milice to fight the French Resistance.

1944   Allied forces land in Normandy in June. Paris is liberated by Allied forces in August. The Vichy government is dissolved, and Pétain is taken to Germany.

1945   Pétain surrenders to French authorities in May, and World War II in Europe ends. Pétain is convicted of treason in August.

1951   Marshal Pétain dies in exile on the Île d'Yeu.

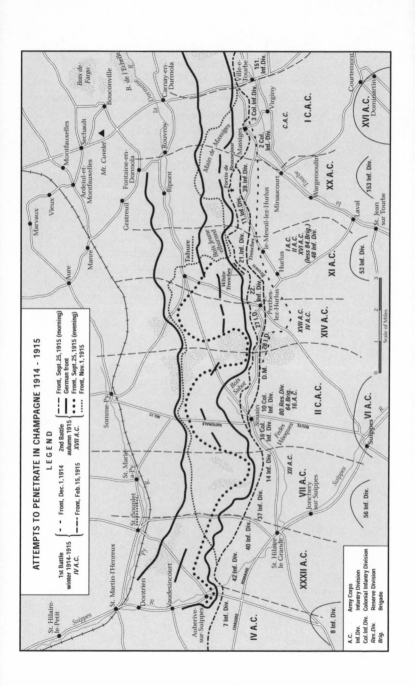

ATTEMPTS TO PENETRATE IN CHAMPAGNE 1914 - 1915

LEGEND

1st Battle
winter 1914-1915
IV A.C.

2nd Battle
autumn 1915
XVII A.C.

{ - - Front, Dec. 1, 1914
{ - - - Front, Feb. 15, 1915

{ -·-· Front, Sept. 25, 1915 (morning)
{ .... German front
{ •••••• Front, Sept. 25, 1915 (evening)
{ ······ Front, Nov. 1, 1915

A.C.   Army Corps
Inf. Div.   Infantry Division
Col. Inf. Div. Colonial Infantry Division
Res. Div.   Reserve Division
Brig.   Brigade

Scale of Miles
0   1   2   3

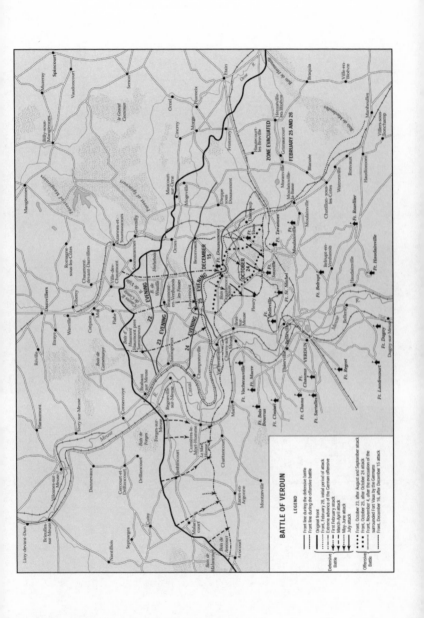

BATTLE OF VERDUN

LEGEND

Defensive Battle
— Front line during the defensive battle
······ Front line during the offensive battle
— Original front
······· Front, February 26, initial period of attack
↑ Extreme advance of the German offensive
↓ First February attack
↓ March–April attack
↓ May–June attack
↓ July attack

Offensive Battle
•••• Front, October 23, after August and September attack
•••• Front, October 25, after October 24 attack
•••• Front, November 4, after the evacuation of the surrounded Fort Vaux by the Germans
—— Front, December 16, after December 15 attack

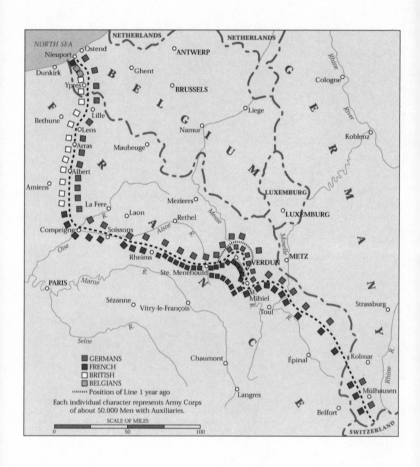

NORTH SEA

NETHERLANDS

NETHERLANDS

ANTWERP

Ostend

Nieuport

Dunkirk

BELGIUM

Ghent

BRUSSELS

Ypres

Lille

Liege

Bethune

Lens

Namur

Arras

Maubeuge

Koblenz

Albert

Amiens

La Fere

Mezieres

LUXEMBURG

Laon

Rethel

LUXEMBURG

Compeigne

Soissons

Rheims

VERDUN

METZ

Ste. Menehould

St. Mihiel

PARIS

Sézanne

Vitry-le-François

Toul

Strassburg

Chaumont

Épinal

Kolmar

GERMANS

FRENCH

BRITISH

BELGIANS

Langres

Mülhausen

••••••• Position of Line 1 year ago

Each individual character represents Army Corps
of about 50,000 Men with Auxiliaries.

Belfort

SWITZERLAND

SCALE OF MILES

0   50   100

The Making of a Soldier, 1856–1914

On March 30, 1856, the cannon at the Hôtel des Invalides in Paris fired a thunderous salute to announce the victory of France and its allies in the Crimean War. The blast from the guns reverberated off the hallowed walls where the mortal remains of Turenne, Vauban, and the great Napoleon were entombed. The cannon fire that echoed through the streets of the French capital signaled to the world that France again stood upon the lofty heights of martial glory and world power, carried there by the French army's bayonets. Napoleon III's Second Empire appeared poised to rival the grandeur and accomplishments of Louis XIV and even Napoleon I. Indeed, France in 1856 was at the pinnacle of power and its army was at the height of its prestige.

Henri Philippe Benoni Omer Pétain (known throughout his life as "Philippe") was born into this France in the small village of Cauchy-à-la-Tour, in the northeastern province of Artois, on April 24, 1856. His father was a farmer who descended from a long line of men who had worked the soil of the same small family plot for more than a century. Pétain's peasant family background was typical as, in spite of the Industrial Revolution that transformed the Western world in the nineteenth century, France was a predominantly agrarian society at the time of Philippe's birth.

Pétain's mother died just before his second birthday. His father re-married about two years later, but the new stepmother did not warm to Philippe or any of the children from the first marriage. This problem became even more acute once she and Philippe's father had their own children. She became increasingly cool and distant to the children of the first marriage, and although they appear to have suffered no physi-cal abuse, Philippe and his siblings were made to feel like strangers in their own home. Philippe's father had little time for him or the other children, and as a consequence, the boy and his father had virtually no relationship whatsoever. Because of this parental neglect, Philippe's deceased mother's parents, who lived nearby, essentially raised him.

In addition to his maternal grandparents, another member of his mother's family became important in Pétain's early life. This was his maternal uncle, the Abbé Legrand, who took a strong interest in all of his late sister's children, especially Philippe. Under Legrand's tutelage the young boy demonstrated an active and curious mind, and Legrand determined that Philippe should have a brighter future than merely work-ing in his father's fields. In 1867, when Philippe was eleven, Legrand arranged to have him sent to Saint-Bertin, a Jesuit school in the village of Saint-Omer, to prepare for a life in which he would use his mind rather than his back to make a living.

At Saint-Bertin, Pétain did well in his studies, but he remained aloof from his fellow classmates and had little patience for those who were not as bright as he was. As a child, Pétain was a loner, serious and taci-turn at an age in life when boys are normally far more carefree. This characteristic dominated his personality throughout his life and was of-ten interpreted by his colleagues, superiors, and later historians as un-reasonable pessimism. While he certainly could be pessimistic at times, he was more often pragmatic and always aware of the dangers, as well as the opportunities, that a particular situation in life could offer. Regard-less, such a serious personality and stern view of life resulted in his friends being few and far between. This lack of companionship did not particu-larly bother him as a child or later in life as an adult.

As Pétain grew into adolescence, the power of France and its army remained in the ascent. A short victorious war over the Austrians in 1859 secured more territory for France, added yet more prestige to French arms, and confirmed the position of the French Empire as the most powerful nation on the continent. The French also began to develop into a truely world power during this time, renewing their former interest in overseas possessions. France had been deeply involved in North Africa since its 1830 invasion of Algeria, but Napoleon III sought wider horizons for his vision of glory and hoped to extend French power and influence throughout the world. To that end, French forces invaded Cochin China in 1860 and, in a series of conflicts over a period of two decades, made themselves the masters of Southeast Asia. French forces, allied with the British, also intervened in the Taiping Rebellion in China and captured Peking in 1861. Finally, in the same year, French forces, taking advantage of internal political turmoil in Mexico and the U.S. Civil War, invaded Mexico and placed Emperor Maximilian on a newly created throne supported by French troops. Shockingly, the glorious Second Empire came crashing to earth in 1870, when Prussia and its German allies swiftly defeated Napoleon III and his vaunted army in a war that shattered the lives of fourteen-year-old Pétain and indeed every person in France.

In the summer of 1870, tension between France and Prussia rose sharply over differences regarding succession to the Spanish throne and Prussian ambitions in the Germanic states. In the midst of this crisis, Prussian chancellor Otto von Bismarck successfully goaded France into declaring war on Prussia on July 15, 1870. The French army, resting on its laurels and blissfully ignorant of the formidable adversary it faced, went to war against Prussia only to find itself heavily outnumbered by an enemy whose ranks had been swelled by soldiers from virtually every German state. Indeed it was a German, and not just a Prussian, army that marched against France that fateful summer. French soldiers fought valiantly in a series of bloody engagements, but they were poorly led by their high command. Napoleon III and his marshals were badly outmaneuvered and severely defeated in the opening campaign that culminated in a resounding defeat for France at Sedan, where the emperor was taken prisoner along with the main French army on September 1, 1870.

A war that had begun with predictions from virtually every foreign observer of a swift French victory had turned out quite differently. In just six weeks, France had lost its emperor and its army, and powerful German forces had marched into the heart of the Second Empire. The news of Napoleon III's defeat sparked a revolution in Paris, and a republic was proclaimed. Galvanized by a return to the republican ideology that had motivated their forefathers to heroic resistance during the French Revolution, the people of France fought on. A *levée en masse* was declared, and civilians were conscripted and hastily trained in a desperate effort to replace the French army that had already been destroyed in the opening weeks of the war. The new French National Army, like its imperial counterpart, fought bravely, but the early defeats and the German isolation of Paris, which was placed under a tight siege, made resistance futile. After a series of failed attempts to break the siege of Paris, the new republic faced the inevitable and sued for peace in January 1871.

The Treaty of Frankfurt that the new German Empire forced on the Third Republic of France in 1871 was a conqueror's peace designed not only to humiliate the proud French but also to permanently cripple the nation as a military power for generations to come. By its terms the Germans annexed the province of Alsace, along with the "German" regions of Lorraine, and foisted war reparations amounting to the largest in the history of European warfare on the defeated French nation. The balance of power in Europe had been irrevocably altered, and the power of France, the most dominant nation on the continent for two centuries, had been eclipsed.

The impact of this national catastrophe on the young Pétain cannot be overstated. Already a patriotic young Frenchman at the tender age of fourteen, he had witnessed the complete downfall of his once mighty nation and its proud army. Thus, it is no coincidence that, shortly after the conclusion of the Franco-Prussian War, Pétain, who until then had been noncommittal about his future, determined that he would seek a career as an officer in the French army. Like many others of his generation, he began to live for *la revanche* (the revenge), the day when the disgrace of this defeat would be erased and France and its army would be restored to their former glory.

After graduating from Saint-Bertin Pétain undertook a year of intensive work at the Dominican collège Albert-le-Grand and then won admission to the elite French military academy of Saint-Cyr in 1876. He demonstrated a keen mind and a strong body at Saint-Cyr. As he grew to manhood he stood almost six feet, with a muscular build. He was handsome and had a shock of blond hair and piercing blue eyes. He graduated from Saint-Cyr with his officer's commission in 1877 as part of the Class of Plevna, named for the battle between Turks and Russians fought in the Balkans that same year. The title was prophetic as the engagement demonstrated the inherent superiority of entrenched rifle and artillery firepower against infantry advancing in the open. This concept remained a pillar of faith with Pétain throughout his military career as he was convinced, at a time when it was not fashionable to be so disposed, that firepower dominated the battlefield with everything else being a secondary consideration.

Pétain entered the infantry and joined an elite *Chasseurs Alpins* regiment. These were mountain troops, trained to fight along France's southeastern frontier with Italy. The physical requirements for serving in these units were demanding, but Pétain readily met the challenge and soon became a skilled mountaineer with a reputation for outstanding courage, physical strength, and endurance. Throughout his life, Pétain maintained himself in superb physical condition, and even in his advanced years he never failed to impress people with his physique and youthful appearance. He spent the next twenty years, off and on, with various Chasseur regiments, and infantry tactics became an obsession for him.

The French viewed the army that Pétain served in from 1877 to 1890 as the living embodiment of the republic. This force would defend France from the foreign invader as she rebuilt her strength and then would serve as the power by which France would one day avenge the defeats of 1870 and retake Alsace and Lorraine. The mission for Pétain, and many other French army officers, was clear: train and prepare every day for the inevitable rematch with the Germans.

Throughout this period, the Third Republic renewed the fallen empire's efforts at colonial expansion. France attempted to regain its power and prestige in the world through military victories overseas and the acquisition of territory in Africa and Asia. By the 1890s, only Britain had a larger overseas empire than France. Many future leaders of the army, such as Joseph Joffre, Hubert Lyautey, and Charles Mangin, found promotion and glory in these colonial campaigns. Pétain, however, never felt the call to war in exotic climes. Instead he remained in Europe, fixated on the only thing that truly mattered in his mind, the inevitable future war with Germany.

Pétain's personal life during this time revolved around a long series of female conquests that were as brief as they were numerous. He loved women but in an almost exclusively sexual context. While he by no means grew wealthy on the pay of an officer in the Third Republic's army, it appears as though it was not his financial situation alone that prevented him from marrying. While professionally he could remain fixated on a single mission, he was not one to devote his personal affections to only one woman. He was handsome and athletic and had a commanding presence, all of which made him attractive to women. He enjoyed these gifts to their fullest advantage.

The French army underwent an odious series of events beginning in 1894. In that year a French intelligence officer who happened to be Jewish, named Alfred Dreyfus, was arrested and charged with selling military secrets to the Germans. He was swiftly convicted and sentenced to life in prison at the notorious prison camp on Devil's Island, off the coast of French Guiana. A scandal erupted when a series of investigations revealed that Dreyfus had been railroaded by corrupt rightist elements in the French army's officer corps. The government eventually pardoned Dreyfus, but the Left was not willing to stop there. It undertook a massive purge to eliminate rightist elements from the French army, and as in all such purges, many loyal and capable French officers were dishonored and forced from the service, many for being nothing more than devout Catholics.

Pétain managed to remain essentially untouched during this massive upheaval. Although he came from a strong Catholic background and had been educated by the Jesuits and the Dominicans, in adulthood he had developed a casual attitude toward his faith and at the time of the scandal had not attended mass in many years. As he came from a peasant background, he had little sympathy for royalists, and this too kept him above suspicion. It should be noted, however, that while he supported the egalitarianism of the Third Republic he did not have much enthusiasm for liberal democratic institutions, but for the most part he kept his thoughts on such matters to himself for many years. Indeed, throughout his early military career Pétain remained apolitical, and not until the First World War did he demonstrate any interest in political matters or publicly voice his opinions regarding the efficacy of the republic in ruling the nation. Military affairs were more interesting for Pétain than the political intrigues of the Third Republic, and in his opinion military matters were also far more important. To Pétain the enemy was the German Empire, and preparations for the future war with France's old nemesis dominated his life throughout his early military career.

The German army was indeed a formidable adversary, and it had grown even stronger in the years since its victory over France in 1871. French military planners had to deal with several sobering facts, not the least of which was that the population of the new German Empire was larger than that of France. By the outbreak of war in 1914 the population of Germany was sixty-eight million, while that of France was approximately forty million. This population base added more recruits to the German army, which had outnumbered the French in the Franco-Prussian War and was even larger now. Thus, the French high command was forced to accept that in the future war with Germany, an early offensive was simply out of the question. The strength of the Germans would have to be broken in a series of defensive engagements before a counteroffensive could ever be launched.

With this defensive battle in mind, the French army began construction of a network of fortresses, under the able direction of Gen. Raymond Adolphe Séré de Rivières, to cauterize the country's torn eastern frontier with the German Empire. The French General Staff hoped that these fortifications would augment the strength of the French army, enabling it to break up the German attacks. With the strength of the enemy broken, the forts would then become a staging area for a counteroffensive that would destroy the invader and move forward to liberate the lost provinces. Yet not every French officer was content to accept such a passive approach to war, and in the latter part of the nineteenth century, a new school of military thought embraced an aggressive military doctrine referred to as the *offensive à outrance*.

This new theory of warfare, sometimes called the "cult of the offensive," had its roots in the French officer corps' obsessive study of the Franco-Prussian War in a search for the causes of their defeat. As they studied the campaigns and battles of 1870–71, one issue seemed to increasingly stand out: the relative passivity of French tactical doctrine during the war's major battles. During the conflict, the French infantry had been equipped with the *chassepot*, one of the finest rifles in the world, and in battle they had routinely assumed defensive positions and then attempted to stop attacking Germans with rifle fire. While the Germans had often suffered heavier battlefield casualties than the French in the war's various engagements, the Germans' ability to outmaneuver the static French formations through aggressive offensive tactics repeatedly defeated the French infantry in battle. This notion that aggressive offensive tactics were superior to defensive firepower was further reinforced when the theorists compared French operations during the Franco-Prussian War with their earlier successful campaigns in Italy and the Crimea. In those conflicts, French infantry doctrine had been more focused on shock tactics and closing with the bayonet than they had been in firefights, and the French had emerged victorious in every engagement.

Taking their studies further back to the dramatic successes of the Napoleonic Wars, the offensive theorists pointed out that, regardless of the overall strategic situation, Napoleon almost always attacked his enemy first. This, they argued, enabled the emperor to seize the initiative and dictate the flow of the battle to his enemy. Indeed, aggressiveness was seen as the hallmark of Napoleon's genius. The offensive à outrance theorists, who included men such as Louis Loizeau de Grandmaison and Ferdinand Foch, concluded that the offensive was a superior form of warfare to the defensive, and that regardless of the overall situation, the best tactical, operational, and strategic solution to any military problem was to attack.

The theorists became almost metaphysical in their discussions of the French soldier's spirit of élan, best demonstrated by wildly aggressive charges with fixed bayonets, which would sweep all before it. Over time these theories increasingly denigrated the role of artillery and even rifle fire as merely secondary considerations or, worse, impediments to the attack. After all, a soldier pausing to fire was not a soldier advancing, and it was in the attack, the new theorists argued, that the French soldier could be in his most effective role as he drove the enemy from the field at the point of his bayonet.

While there was some logic to the theories of the adherents of the cult of the offensive, their studies failed to take into account vital information from their historical examples. While it was true that French infantry in the Franco-Prussian War had relied on defensive firepower, it had rarely dug entrenchments or even taken full advantage of the terrain available to it. Thus, in practice, its positions were far less formidable than they could have been. In addition, German artillery had overwhelmed the defensive firepower generated by French rifles. The German guns were more numerous and fired heavier shells more accurately and over longer ranges than their French counterparts. Exposed infantry, pounded at long range by heavy artillery, became quite vulnerable indeed, especially when they were seriously outnumbered by their German opponents in virtually every battle and thus were routinely flanked. Yet rather than focusing on how defensive tactics could be improved, and in particular on how entrenchments and heavy artillery could be utilized on the modern battlefield, the cult of the offensive theorists dismissed all defensive tactics as timid and defeatist.

Pétain was one of the few French officers not enamored by the offensive à outrance theorists. Instead he adhered to the more established principles of the French army's senior leadership, which realized that the strategic position of France was ill-suited for offensive warfare against Germany. At the tactical level, Pétain was obsessed with firepower, and in his various assignments, he relentlessly drilled his men in marksmanship and the use of rifle fire to support the advance. Pétain dismissed the notion of the mystical spirit of élan popular among his peers as little more than metaphysical musings that were at best ridiculous and at worst dangerous. In Pétain's view, firepower, not high-spirited men with bayonets, dominated the modern battlefield. The only way an advance could be made or a defense maintained, he argued, was to attain fire superiority over the enemy. Every other consideration was tangential to this basic fact, and all the fanatical bravery in the world could not alone win against modern weapons in the hands of trained soldiers. He developed a simple phrase *le feu tue* (fire kills) and stressed this concept to his soldiers.

Pétain also studied military history, in particular the Napoleonic Wars of 1796 to 1815. In so doing, he came to completely different conclusions regarding the secret of the great Napoleon's victories. While offensive à outrance theorists emphasized wild bayonet charges, Pétain focused on the emperor's use of a "grand battery" of artillery to establish fire supremacy over the area of the battlefield chosen for an attack. Indeed, for Pétain, Napoleon's recognition of the supremacy of firepower was the secret of his tactical genius. Pétain argued that modern small arms and machine guns further enhanced an army's ability to generate fire on the battlefield and that in the modern age infantry firepower should be welded together with the artillery to achieve fire supremacy. In his view, a defending force that possessed fire superiority could not be overcome, but an attacking force possessing such an advantage would be unstoppable. Thus, the critical factor to be emphasized at every level, and in every mission, was fire superiority.

Had he managed to keep his counsel on military affairs, he may have risen rapidly in rank during the decades preceding the Great War, but Pétain developed strong opinions on military matters and did not hesitate to voice his views regardless of the consequences. His opinions on infantry tactics and his belief in the supreme role of firepower on the modern battlefield placed him in direct opposition to most of the officers of his generation, who became obsessed with the offensive à outrance and the superiority of moral factors in warfare.

Pétain was highly respected and well liked by his subordinates, and his professionalism and leadership abilities marked him for early promotion. However, his penchant for speaking his mind to his superiors, regardless of the situation, routinely sabotaged his career. He was not one to stand on politeness if he believed he was right and the other individual wrong, even if the other person happened to outrank him. Pétain could be blunt, sometimes painfully so, and spoke his mind freely, as if he were oblivious to the impact his words could have on others or on his career.

In spite of this troublesome personality trait, Pétain was well respected for his abilities as an officer and for his theories on firepower and consequently was promoted to major and appointed to the faculty of the École de Tir at Châlons in 1900. The appointment was a wonderful opportunity for Pétain to take his theories to a wider audience and perhaps even begin to stem the tide of the cult of the offensive that had become so prevalent in the French officer corps. Yet he had hardly settled into his new post when his brusque personality brought him into conflict with the school's director, Colonel Vonderscherr. The director was a man who did things "by the book," and Pétain's novel ideas on infantry tactics and coordination of firepower did not conform to regulations, inspired by the new offensive doctrine, laid down by the French army.

At the École de Tir, Vonderscherr emphasized tactics more suitable for Napoleon's soldiers than for twentieth-century servicemen. His view of infantry battle involved men firing by volley at a general area, producing a "cone of fire" to maximize the chance of hitting something. After a few volleys, bugles would sound the advance and a wild bayonet charge would ensue that would theoretically sweep all before it. Pétain saw such tactics as outmoded and even foolish given the killing power of modern weapons. He immediately rejected this curriculum and instead drilled his men relentlessly on individual marksmanship rather than area fire by volley. He also stressed that accurate and sustained rifle fire was essential throughout every moment of infantry battle, including during the attack, when it was far more effective to have a steady advance by firing riflemen than a bayonet charge.

Pétain's refusal to adhere to the approved curriculum for the school brought swift rebukes from Vonderscherr, but Pétain shrugged off these reprimands and continued to teach his methods to the soldiers. The two men had repeated quarrels over the matter, with Pétain refusing to back down, until at last his intransigence led to his dismissal from the school after just six months. The two men would not meet again until shortly after the Great War, during which Pétain's theories on the importance of firepower were proved to be prophecy rather than heresy. Vonderscherr, now a general, saluted his former subordinate, now a marshal of France, and said, "At Châlons, it was Major Pétain who had reason."[1]

In 1901, shortly after his dismissal from the École de Tir, Pétain was appointed a professor of infantry tactics at the prestigious École de Guerre in Paris. There he remained a loner and, though seen as an outsider, nevertheless attracted a small but dedicated group of followers. Pétain also, at this time, began to seriously consider the prospect of marriage.

Pétain had been a confirmed bachelor his whole life, but his new position promised to open up a world of respectability and domesticity in Paris. He was forty-five years old and the prospect of settling down to a life of married bliss was more appealing to him than it had been as young man. He therefore decided to make his first genuine attempt at marriage. Although many years had passed, he had not forgotten the beautiful and charming young Eugénie Hardon, whom he had first met in 1881, when she was just four. He had maintained contact with her family over the years, and he became infatuated with the young woman once she reached adulthood.

Convinced that his new position as a professor at the École de Guerre would be prestigious enough to meet the stern requirements for stability and respectability that her parents demanded, he decided to ask for her hand in marriage. While Eugénie was enamored with the handsome officer, her family strongly disapproved of the match. Pétain was after all twenty-one years her senior, and her father was apparently aware of his reputation as a womanizer. M. Hardon also disapproved of Pétain's profession, which did not promise the stability he wanted for his daughter or the economic windfall that he hoped to bring to the family through the marriage of his daughter to a more appropriate, and more affluent, gentleman. In spite of several gallant attempts by Pétain to win the Hardon family's approval, he was forcefully met with rejection by Eugénie's parents.

Stung by this rebuke, Pétain broke ties with the Hardon family and abandoned his pursuit of Eugénie, he thought for good. He later stated that shortly after this failed attempt at romance he made a final determination that his family was the army and resolved to dedicate his life to serving France. While there is no reason to doubt Pétain's sincerity in this remark, it should be noted that he did continue to pursue women, albeit for far less noble intentions than marriage, and his numerous romantic liaisons did not distract him from his duties or his service to France.

Pétain served as a professor at the École de Guerre from 1901 to 1911, with occasional assignments to various infantry regiments mixed in. He taught infantry tactics, and his theories on firepower and open contempt for the doctrine of offensive à outrance made him an outcast among his fellow instructors. In addition to his work on infantry tactics, Pétain also labored to develop better coordination between the infantry and artillery, a subject that had been almost completely neglected by the French high command yet one that he believed was an essential component of modern warfare. Artillery and infantry officers rarely held joint training sessions, and artillerists had become inclined to view their role as waging an almost separate battle rather than providing supporting fire to the infantry. In Pétain's view the two branches had to be welded together into a team as artillery support was a vital prerequisite for the infantry, whether on the attack or defense, and this combination was an integral part of his theories regarding the establishment of fire supremacy on the battlefield.

While Pétain's novel tactical theories and bluntness won him a small circle of followers, his habit of speaking whatever was on his mind and his complete lack of deference to superior officers also made him many enemies. During the prewar maneuvers held in the autumn of 1913, three regiments under the overall command of General Le Gallet, Pétain's immediate superior, staged an attack on what was supposed to be a fortified "enemy-held village on a hilltop. No artillery preparation was used, but regimental bands were in full cry. The colors were unfurled with great ceremony, and officers with drawn sabers took their posts at the front of their men as they gave the order to fix bayonets. Without a single volley being fired, the buglers sounded the charge, officers shouted, "*En avant!*" and the regiments swept up the slope, their banners snapping in the breeze. The regimental bands played their stirring marches throughout the course of the advance, which culminated in the "capture" of the village at bayonet point. It was dramatic, it was inspiring, and it had a martial beauty and grace scarcely rivaled. Yet, as Marshal Bosquest had commented on the charge of the Light Brigade in the Crimea, "It is magnificent, but it is not war."

The commanding general of the division was visibly impressed with the spirit and dash shown by the men and the impressive spectacle the maneuver had provided. The brigade commander, General Le Gallet, was heaped with praise, and then it was noticed that Pétain had not spoken a word, and so he was asked for his impressions of the affair. With the acidic wit for which he was well known, Pétain responded, "I am sure that General Le Gallet intended, the better to impress you, to present a synthesis of all the mistakes that a modern army should not commit." The circle of jubilant officers suddenly fell silent as everyone turned in amazement toward this brazen regimental commander. Pétain continued, "Let us first crush the enemy by artillery fire, and afterwards we shall win our victory."[2]

The incident was typical of Pétain's prewar career, and these sorts of disputes with superiors and his stubborn refusal to accept current trends in military tactics were the main reason he was routinely passed over for promotion by lesser men who either accepted the fashionable theories in military thinking or, if they did not, had the sense to keep their mouths shut. This experience naturally engendered in Pétain some bitterness, which exacerbated his irascible personality traits. As far as he was concerned, he knew he was right and those who disagreed with him were wrong. While that fact caused great consternation it did not cause him to rethink his positions.

Unfortunately for Pétain, and indeed for the whole French army, by 1911 he had lost his battle with the theorists of the offensive à outrance. In that year, he was banished from the École de Guerre and reassigned to command of the Thirty-third Infantry Regiment. The cult of the offensive adherents soon held absolute sway at virtually all levels of the French army and even succeeded in having one of their own, Gen. Joseph Joffre, appointed commander in chief of the army. The new infantry regulations adopted that year reflected this overwhelming influence as practical application of modern weaponry was thrown out in favor of the bayonet and the *furia française* (French Fury).

Even though he was now an outcast and heretic in the eyes of the senior officers, Pétain retained a small but devoted circle of followers who respected his thoughts on tactics and revered him for his courage in speaking his mind and standing up for his beliefs regardless of the consequences. The fact that his theories were controversial and flew in the face of accepted doctrine attracted a new generation of younger officers eager to make their mark and ready to reject the accepted wisdom of the cult of the offensive.

Among these early followers of Pétain was a young lieutenant named Charles de Gaulle, whose destiny would be inextricably entwined with that of Pétain. De Gaulle learned about Pétain and his heretical views on battlefield tactics while studying at Saint-Cyr and was immediately taken in. When Pétain was reassigned from the École de Guerre to take command of the Thirteenth Infantry Regiment, de Gaulle requested to be assigned to this regiment in order to study the art of war with a man he considered to be an avant-garde genius. Pétain did not fail to impress, and de Gaulle soon became a devoted follower, learning everything he could from the man he idolized. He eagerly imitated Pétain's blunt, no-nonsense approach and also adopted his lack of deference to authority and his disrespect for any officer who failed to accept or understand the new ways of war. As they did for his mentor, these personality traits served to both aid and detract from de Gaulle's career, and there can be no question that his early association with Pétain left a lasting mark on the young officer.

Yet while Pétain retained the respect and admiration of his men, his bitter duels with the cult of the offensive theorists continued to plague his career even after he had left the École de Guerre. In 1913 his friend and supporter Gen. Louis Franchet d'Esperey recommended Colonel Pétain for promotion to *général de brigade* and command of the Fourth Infantry Brigade of the Sixth Infantry Division. The War Ministry could not deny an army commander the right to assign a brigade command, and he was appointed to his new post without delay. However, his enemies at the ministry blocked Pétain's promotion to general officer rank.

Colonel Pétain was now fifty-seven and faced mandatory retirement in just two years' time. Indeed, it appeared that Pétain's long military career had come to an uneventful end and that he would soon retire on his pension, leaving the field to his intellectual adversaries whose reshaping of French army doctrine meant that his long struggle for a rational approach to the modern battlefield had met with defeat. In early 1914, he made arrangements to purchase a small farm in his native Artois, where he hoped to spend his twilight years, and prepared to retire from active service. Then came the dramatic summer of that apocalyptic year, and Pétain's life was forever changed.

Heretic to Prophet:
The 1914 & 1915 Campaigns

A terrorist armed and trained by agents within the Serbian army assassinated Archduke Franz Ferdinand, heir to the throne of Austria-Hungary, on June 28, 1914. This incident in the Balkans catapulted the most powerful nations on earth into the largest war yet seen in human history. As Austro-Hungarian forces massed for a punitive war against Serbia, Russia responded by mobilizing its armed forces to protect Serbia and safeguard its own interests in the Balkans. Germany responded by backing its ally Austria-Hungary, and France was suddenly forced to decide on whether to support its ally Russia. Understanding that without her powerful eastern partner France would be forced to face the full might of Germany in any future war alone, French president Raymond Poincaré offered his government's full support to Russia in the crisis. When Germany declared war on Russia on August 1, 1914, France responded by ordering a general mobilization of the army. Germany then declared war on France as well, and thus the Great War had begun.

Known as Plan XVII, the overall French plan of operations had been designed by the cult of the offensive theorists and adopted by the French commander in chief, Gen. Joseph Joffre, in 1913. Unlike earlier war plans that had envisioned an initially defensive posture for the French army, Plan XVII called for an immediate attack into Lorraine and Alsace on the outbreak of hostilities. The ultimate goal was the liberation of the provinces lost in the Franco-Prussian War by defeating the main German army in a massive head-on collision.

When the war broke out Pétain commanded the Fourth Brigade of the Second Infantry Division, which was part of Gen. Charles Lanrezac's Fifth Army. The Fifth Army anchored the left flank of the four French armies that were slated to attack into Alsace and Lorraine. As the French army began to concentrate on the coming offensive on August 14, Lanrezac moved his army northeast into Belgium and bumped into a powerful German cavalry screen. Lanrezac had never been enamored with the offensive à outrance doctrine, and since his mission was to protect the flank of the main offensive, he deployed his army into defensive positions along the Meuse River.

Pétain's brigade was assigned to hold a low ridge overlooking the Meuse near the Belgian village of Anhée. He moved his artillery batteries forward into somewhat exposed positions to provide direct supporting fire to his infantry. The batteries were composed exclusively of the famous *soixante-quinze*, the M1903 75 mm gun whose high rate of fire, accuracy, and maneuverability made it the darling of the French high command. Although a superb light gun, it was a direct-fire weapon, and thus the gunners were forced to take up forward positions to effectively use their pieces. While the French 75 mm field gun was superior to its counterpart, the German 77 mm field gun, it could not match the range and firepower of the German 150 mm howitzers, batteries of which accompanied every German division and could rain down heavier shells from a safe distance using indirect-fire methods perfected before the war. At this stage of the conflict, the French field armies had virtually no heavy artillery and were forced to use their 75 mm guns for all fire missions.

On August 15 Pétain's brigade was hit with repeated German attacks as the enemy attempted to force his way across the Meuse. Pétain handled his brigade well during this three-day battle, and he displayed a courage and indifference to danger throughout the action that he repeated often during this early stage of the war. His officers and men constantly saw him on the front line, and he often went right up to the scene of action to encourage his troops. He did this not merely for morale purposes, however. After decades of theoretical debate on infantry tactics, he wanted to see firsthand how his ideas would play out, and his command presence was matched by a scholar's determination to learn the truth of modern battle. In this respect he was not content to merely observe the results of his own actions but was also quick to interrogate officers and soldiers from neighboring units as to their battlefield experiences, in particular the effect that artillery and machine guns were having on the conduct of the battle. In each case his notions of firepower's supremacy on the battlefield were confirmed; however, his views remained very much in the minority when on August 20 General Joffre, with his forces fully deployed and ready for action, ordered an all-out offensive into Lorraine and Alsace.

While there was nothing wrong in principle with an aggressive strategy, the breakdown occurred, as Pétain had warned for years, at the tactical level. Élan was not enough to overcome machine guns and was in fact a poor substitute for proper tactical doctrine. As the French army went on the attack in those opening weeks of the war, regimental commanders routinely ordered bayonet charges and rarely waited for their artillery to even deploy, never mind shell the chosen area of attack with preparatory fire. Instead the French infantrymen surged to the attack wearing their famous bright red trousers and kepis, their regimental colors snapping in the air as their bands played stirring songs from the Napoleonic Wars. All of the flaws of the *offensive à outrance* tactics that Pétain had warned about for decades were now enacted in deadly earnest as French regiments rushed forward with fixed bayonets against German machine guns supported by heavy artillery. All along the line the French attacks were checked and then hurled backward after suffering catastrophic casualties.

As the French offensive bogged down, the main German attack began to develop in the north. Following the basic tenets of the Schlieffen Plan, Gen. Helmuth von Moltke sent five German armies hurtling through neutral Belgium in a gigantic flanking movement around the French army. French Grand Quartier Général (GQG) was slow to react as its intelligence service had dramatically underestimated the German army's overall strength and intentions. Not until German forces captured Brussels and were crossing the Meuse River in great strength did Joffre realize the dangerous situation he was in. He made an effort to pivot part of his offensive northward by ordering elements of Lanrezac's Fifth Army to strike the flank of the onrushing Germans, yet this effort too met with defeat because of poor tactics.

By August 24 Joffre's offensive had collapsed, and large numbers of German troops were pouring around his armies' northern flank while French forces in the south began to fall back in disarray. Joffre ordered a general withdrawal to commence immediately in the hopes of breaking contact with the Germans and reestablishing solid defensive positions somewhere deeper in France's interior. As Lanrezac's Fifth Army joined the retreat, he ordered his I Corps to cover the withdrawal, and Pétain's brigade was given a prominent role in this desperate rearguard action. Pétain carried out his assignment brilliantly, executing a series of defensive stands that repeatedly bloodied the pursuing Germans, slowing their advance, and buying valuable time for the rest of Fifth Army.

As the French army fell back toward Paris, Joffre began to restore order to his shattered forces. First he nearly decapitated the French command structure, dismissing one senior commander after another, including General Lanrezac. Fortunately for Pétain, Lanrezac was replaced by Pétain's corps commander General d'Esperey, who shared Lanrezac's high opinion of their outspoken brigade commander. It will be recalled that d'Esperey had attempted to promote Pétain to general officer rank prior to the war. Now, thanks to Pétain's splendid performance in the war's early battles and the massive upheaval caused by Joffre's housecleaning, the way was at last clear for his well-deserved promotion.

While resting at the home of a small farming family that served as his temporary brigade headquarters on the night of August 28, Pétain received orders promoting him to the rank of général de brigade. The lady of the house was the daughter of Gen. Henri de Sonis, a hero of the wars of the Second Empire. On hearing of her guest's promotion, she took out her father's old uniform, removed its general's stars, and sewed them onto Pétain's uniform. The following morning she presented the uniform to Pétain with tears in her eyes and told him that she hoped they would bring him and France great fortune in the desperate days ahead. The stars Pétain had longed for were at last his, but as the commander of a bedraggled rear guard protecting a retreating army in the midst of a campaign whose issue was in doubt, he could find no great joy in his promotion.

General d'Esperey had barely assumed command when he turned his Fifth Army around and launched a surprising counteroffensive against the pursuing Germans near the village of Guise on August 29, 1914. The brigades went forward with all the precepts of the *offensive à outrance* still intact, attacking in dense formations while desperately trying to close on their enemies with the bayonet. Pétain, whose brigade would attack last, watched them go out with a professional disdain that turned to horror as he saw their shattered ranks tumbling back scarcely an hour later. His own men were clearly rattled by the spectacle, but Pétain mounted his horse and rode through the ranks restoring morale while at the same time spreading his troops out into a proper attack formation. Just before night fell, he at last received the order to go forward. In the fading twilight, he organized his artillery batteries to lay down a powerful barrage on the enemy lines, and then, determined to make sure the proper tactics were employed, he personally accompanied one of his regiments in the assault. His brigade made good headway, but night fell before he could completely achieve his objectives and his battalions became confused and mixed in the darkness.

After spending most of the night reorganizing his brigade to renew the assault in the morning, orders came that the Fifth Army was once more breaking contact and withdrawing. Pétain's brigade was once more given the task of serving as the army's rear guard. The reasons for the decision to withdraw were complex, but in part it was because d'Esperey had been unable, as had Lanrezac before him, to coordinate his actions with the British Expeditionary Force (BEF), which was supposed to be supporting French operations. Pétain reported bitterly on the British failure to support his forces, and the incident appears to have had a lasting effect upon his character. Prior to this action, it is doubtful that Pétain thought much one way or the other regarding the British, but after the engagement, and the British failure to come to his aid, he developed an increasingly Anglophobe streak to his character that grew stronger throughout his life.

After three days of desperate fighting and hard marching, a command car from Fifth Army headquarters roared up to Pétain's haggard command post, sending a swirl of choking dust into the air. A staff officer jumped out to inform Pétain that he had been promoted to command the Sixth Infantry Division and was to report there immediately. Word of the heretic general and his views on firepower—which were being proved all too prophetic on the battlefield—was spreading rapidly through the French army. Yet again, Pétain could take only cold comfort in this because the French army had suffered enormous casualties before others had reached this conclusion. As in 1870, the French army had suffered a devastating defeat along the eastern frontier. However, unlike the French high command in the Franco-Prussian War, Joffre had managed to extricate his armies from their potentially deadly predicament and was determined to turn and make a stand before Paris along the Marne River.

Pétain took command of the Sixth Division in the midst of Joffre's general withdrawal on September 2, 1914. He found his new command to be exhausted and demoralized and in an almost chaotic state in terms of its discipline. Rallying a shattered division was an arduous task under any circumstances, but to do so in the midst of a losing campaign while in full retreat before a powerful enemy force was truly daunting. Yet that is exactly what Pétain did. He shook up the command structure of the division, relieving several officers he deemed incompetent or who had lost their men's respect. He also undertook personal visits to his battalions and was a visible presence among his men, encouraging them with kind words but also enforcing discipline. When his exhausted division crossed to the Marne's south bank, many men broke ranks to pillage a fruit orchard alongside the road. A furious Pétain drew his revolver and spurred his horse into the orchard firing shots into the air. He then barked harsh orders to the startled soldiers, telling them to reform on the road or face the consequences of their actions. The looters swiftly obeyed, and the men of the Sixth Division came away from the incident impressed that their new commanding general was a man who meant business. Pétain had little time in which to complete his division's refitting before the decisive moment of the campaign arrived.

The German advance had begun to lose momentum in early September, and the German right wing, which consisted of Gen. Alexander von Kluck's First Army and Gen. Karl von Bülow's Second Army, had become precariously overextended in their dash toward Paris. Von Kluck's First Army had turned south in front of Paris, instead of enveloping it as originally planned, exposing its right flank to French forces in the capital, and the two German armies had failed to keep in close contact, leaving them vulnerable to a counterstroke. With the enemy a scant forty miles from Paris, Joffre readied his battered French army for a massive counterstroke. The French Sixth Army would attack out of Paris against von Kluck's right flank, and General d'Esperey's Fifth Army, supported by Gen. Sir John French's British Expeditionary Force, would attack into the gap between the German First and Second armies.

D'Esperey chose Pétain's division to spearhead the Fifth Army's assault. On the day of the attack, Pétain had his batteries of 75 mm field guns lay down an intense barrage of fire on the enemy lines to his front while ordering his overly aggressive battalion and regimental commanders (still under the influence of the *offensive à outrance* theories) not to advance until he issued a personal command to do so. After several hours of artillery fire, Pétain unleashed his infantry, and it surged forward into a hail of German machine-gun and rifle fire. After a brief advance the attack faltered, as the men went to ground and refused to move forward. Much to their astonishment, Pétain suddenly appeared on the front line, and the men rallied to him. Pétain led them with drawn revolver, urging them to fire as they advanced, and the attack began to move forward once more. His lead battalions attacked the elite German Sixth "Brandenburg" Division, and a vicious close-range battle was fought. The engagement was sharply contested and casualties were high on both sides, but after three days of intense fighting the Germans were forced to yield their ground. Pétain was constantly at the scene of action throughout the Battle of the Marne, riding on horseback from point to point on the battlefield, as he coordinated his attacking battalions and maneuvered the divisional artillery forward to provide fire support to his infantry.

In testimony to Pétain's leadership and tactical abilities, the French Sixth Division, which had performed abysmally at the Battle of Guise just two weeks earlier, was magnificent at the Battle of the Marne. The battle played a significant role in the French Fifth Army's successful attack against the German lines along the Petit Morin River. Faced with the potential isolation and destruction of two entire German armies, General von Moltke ordered a strategic withdrawal of German forces away from Paris, thus ending any hope for a swift German victory in the war. A furious Kaiser Wilhelm II summarily relieved von Moltke of command and replaced him with Gen. Erich von Falkenhayn.

Under their new commander, the Germans continued their withdrawal until they had extricated themselves from their previously dire predicament. Then Falkenhayn ordered local counterattacks to slow the onrushing Allied forces. On September 13, Pétain's division was suddenly struck by savage counterattacks that took him completely by surprise. He quickly recovered his balance, however, and revealed a talent for rapid improvisation on the battlefield. He also demonstrated a ferocious tenacity on defense as his division hurled back repeated German assaults. In recognition of his achievements at the Marne and in these battles, Pétain was promoted to the rank of *général de division*, the highest rank in the French army at that time.

Pétain's Sixth Infantry Division continued to push north of the Marne. During the latter part of September the division was engaged in a series of swirling battles to the south and west of Reims in which each side attacked and counterattacked during two weeks of nonstop battle. Once more, it seemed that Pétain was everywhere on the battlefield, and his men grew to greatly admire their brash division commander. By the time the fighting had died down, the front in this sector stabilized. Though the Germans still held a large area of northern and eastern France, they had been pushed well back from their deep penetration south of the Marne, and the French had firmly established a solid defensive line extending from Reims to the north and west that barred another advance on Paris. Pétain's superiors were greatly impressed by his outstanding performance on the battlefield, and honors were rained down on him. In October 1914 he received the *Légion d'honneur*, France's highest award for military service and bravery on the field of battle and was promoted to command of the French XXXIII Corps, attached to Gen. Louis Ernest de Maud'huy's Tenth Army, which was moving north toward Artois.

In the wake of the Battle of the Marne, both the Allied and German armies aggressively maneuvered their forces northward in an attempt to turn the other's flank. This so-called race to the sea ended in a draw when each side reached the English Channel. Undeterred, General Falkenhayn made an attempt to break through the Allied lines in the north at the First Battle of Ypres in November but was turned back with heavy losses by a combined Anglo-French force. After this defeat, Falkenhayn ordered a suspension of offensive operations in the west. Winter was on its way, his armies were exhausted, and their supplies were low, so he commanded his forces to construct a fortified defensive line along commanding terrain to hold the areas of northeastern France and Belgium, which had been won in the initial campaign. This German line would stretch more than three hundred miles from the English Channel to the Swiss Alps and would become infamous as the "Western Front."

General Joffre was not content to allow the Germans to remain masters of their conquests through the winter. Facing considerable political pressure to liberate France's lost territory, he made plans to launch a major offensive at the earliest possible date. Although by this time he realized he would be facing entrenched enemy forces, Joffre was convinced that he could smash his way through the German lines. In addition, he felt it imperative that he keep pressure on the Germans to prevent them from shifting forces to the east, where a winter campaign was raging and France's Russian ally was being pushed to the limit. After some deliberation Joffre chose de Maud'huy's Tenth Army to launch an attack in Artois.

On December 17 the Tenth Army attacked. It was supported by the fire of 632 artillery pieces, of which 110 were heavy guns. The battle opened with preliminary attacks by the XX Corps intended to soften up the enemy and prepare the way for Pétain's XXXIII Corps, which was the main strike force, to deliver the coup de grâce. The initial attack by XX Corps made little headway however. The weather, a mixture of freezing rain and snow, was awful and turned the battlefield into a quagmire that slowed the troops' advance. French artillery support proved to be woefully insufficient, and the brief preliminary bombardment barely scratched the mass of barbed wire in front of the German lines.

After twenty-four hours of battle with little to show for the effort, de Maud'huy sent Pétain's XXXIII Corps into the fray. Much to everyone's surprise this powerful attack floundered as well and could not get the advance moving. Determined to salvage the situation, Pétain decided that the broad breakthrough envisioned by Joffre was impossible, so he reorganized his attack force to concentrate on certain critical objectives. In this fashion he managed to penetrate some seven hundred meters into the German lines, but after suffering heavy casualties, he found it impossible to hold even this small gain against determined German counterattacks. As a consequence, within just a few days his divisions had been knocked practically all the way back to their jump-off point, and the battle had become a desultory affair of attrition waged in mud and snow. On January 15, 1915, Joffre at last admitted defeat and called off the battle.

The lesson that Pétain took from this defeat was that a major adjustment had to be made in terms of envisioning how much artillery fire was necessary to provide proper support for an offensive. Shortly after the battle, Pétain requested that his XXXIII Corps be reinforced with additional artillery batteries and concluded that future offensives must concentrate on realistic tactical objectives rather than broad sweeping strategic movements.

The fighting tapered off on the Western Front for the duration of the winter while the Germans focused on operations in the east and Joffre beefed up his forces for a major operation in the spring. General French's BEF was also heavily reinforced that winter, and Joffre planned to coordinate his attack with an assault by the British in order to place the maximum strain on German defenses. As the weather warmed, the British and French launched their offensives in northern France, with the British attacking Aubers Ridge near Neuve Chapelle, while the French Tenth Army, now under the command of Gen. Victor d'Urbal, attacked in Artois with the mission of seizing Vimy Ridge.

Joffre believed Vimy Ridge was the linchpin in the German defenses in the north and thought that its capture could result in a massive breakthrough of the German lines. In an attempt to learn from past mistakes, he supported this attack with almost twice as many guns as had been used in the previous battle and ordered General d'Urbal to pound the enemy positions to his front for four full days before the attack. After the preparatory bombardment lifted, the French infantry charged forward on May 9, 1915. Yet in spite of the additional preparation fire, the Germans' defenses, especially their barbed wire, remained largely intact and heavy machine-gun fire ripped the lead assault battalions to shreds.

On the left flank of the Tenth Army's offensive the French XXI Corps made only minimal gains before it was stopped cold, while on the right the XX Corps made somewhat better progress before it too bogged down amid determined German resistance and heavy casualties. Yet just as Joffre and d'Urbal began to despair, reports arrived that Pétain's XXXIII Corps had burst through the German defenses in the center and surged up and over Vimy Ridge. In just a few hours of heavy fighting, Pétain's lead regiments advanced more than four kilometers and achieved a clean breakthrough of the German defenses.

The main reason for Pétain's success had been his meticulous planning of the operation as well as his commitment to establishing a close liaison between the infantry and artillery. His batteries kept shells raining down on the German front lines even as the infantry advanced, and his gunners manhandled their 75 mm guns forward to continue to provide direct-fire support against enemy bunkers and fortifications. Each regiment's movement had been methodically scripted with contingency plans for every foreseeable problem that could confront the advance. As a consequence the attack had been launched with a superb coordination between the combat arms and an almost parade-ground smoothness to the assault battalions's movements.

Yet this brilliant success proved to be short lived. The Germans skillfully sealed the breach in their lines and rushed reinforcements to the endangered sector. Because neither of his neighboring corps had made much headway at all, Pétain's advance had left his divisions in a dangerously exposed salient. He urgently requested reinforcements, but unfortunately d'Urbal had placed the Tenth Army's reserves too far to the rear to keep them out of range of German artillery, and thus they were not readily available to exploit the breakthrough. As Pétain waited in vain for reinforcements, German forces began to build up on his flanks. That afternoon the Germans launched counterattacks against his exposed flanks, and the salient began to crumble. In danger of being cut off and annihilated, he reluctantly ordered a tactical withdrawal in order to place his forces back in contact with the Tenth Army's other corps. By nightfall Pétain's XXXIII Corps had been forced to relinquish almost half of its conquered ground, including Vimy Ridge, leaving it just two kilometers deep in the enemy lines.

Although ultimately unsuccessful, Pétain had won a clear tactical victory that day. In addition to breaking completely through the German defense line, his forces had inflicted heavy casualties on the German defenders, capturing more than one thousand prisoners as well as numerous artillery pieces and machine guns. Joffre named Pétain a commander of the Legion of Honor, and Pétain's reputation as one of the premier tacticians in the French army grew exponentially.

Although the Tenth Army's attack had failed, Joffre was encouraged by Pétain's success and ordered the offensive resumed the following day. However, the Germans had been heavily reinforced, and they repulsed one French assault after another. The initial momentum of May 9 was now gone, and once more the battle became one of attrition as successive French attacks throughout May and into June produced few tangible gains while casualties soared to more than 100,000. Joffre grew frustrated, but clung to Pétain's initial tactical success as proof that the German trench line could be broken. What was needed, he believed, was to take *la méthode Pétain* and apply it to a massive offensive, which would attack along a broad front in order to produce a general rupture of the German defensive lines and force the fighting back out into the open.[1]

Joffre viewed Pétain as one of his finest commanders, and on June 21, 1915, he promoted Pétain to command of the French Second Army. The promotion marked yet another milestone in a suddenly meteoric career. Yet for all of his newly won fame and respect for his methods, Pétain had lost none of the gruff frankness that had been a hallmark of his personality throughout his career. This was soon evidenced when Joffre solicited his senior commanders, including Pétain, for their opinions on where they thought the new offensive should be launched. Much to Joffre's surprise, Pétain replied by criticizing the concept of a "breakthrough" offensive. Even though Joffre was loudly trumpeting his corps' success as proof that the German trenches could be broken, the fighting in Artois had brought Pétain to a far different conclusion as to how the war should be fought. The new Second Army commander told Joffre, "The war has become a war of attrition. There will be no decisive battle as in other times. Success will come eventually to the side that has the last man."[2]

Instead of a massive offensive aimed at achieving a breakthrough, Pétain argued for a series of smaller attacks. These attacks would be aimed at vulnerable points in the German line with the intent of inflicting the maximum number of casualties on the Germans rather than gaining ground. In this way, Pétain believed the Germans could be slowly bled to the point of exhaustion and only then would victory be achieved. Such an approach was unacceptable to Joffre at a number of levels. Besides his own firm belief that only a great battle could produce decisive results, he also had political pressures to deal with. Large areas of France had fallen to the Germans, and the government was demanding their swift liberation. An open-ended strategy of attrition with no tangible goal and no timetable for success was simply unacceptable. Joffre rejected Pétain's recommendations out of hand and began to prepare the largest French offensive of the war to take place in Champagne that autumn. Joffre's decision to assign Pétain's Second Army a critical role in the coming offensive was evidence of his continued confidence in his outspoken subordinate.

Interestingly, the Germans had also taken notice of Pétain. German military intelligence had made note of his breakthrough of their trench system in Artois and of his rising reputation within the French army. As a consequence, French intelligence reported to Joffre that the Germans were paying particular attention to Pétain's movements and assignments as an indicator of where the next offensive might take place. Consequently, the French undertook a number of subterfuges to keep the Germans guessing, including sending Pétain on well-publicized visits to various sectors of the line and not officially releasing news of his elevation to command the Second Army until the eve of the great offensive.[3]

Between June and September 1915, the French army began a larg buildup of forces in Champagne and simultaneously underwent a major transformation as a fighting force. During this time the French soldier was issued a new *horizon bleu* uniform and steel helmet to replace the nineteenth-century red trousers and kepi. At the same time the army was equipped with more and larger pieces of artillery than ever before. Joffre assembled approximately 5,000 artillery pieces for the offensive, including more than 2,000 heavy (90 mm and larger) guns. This was now a thoroughly modern fighting force that had been tried and tested on the battlefield for longer than a year, and by September Joffre believed it was ready for the most ambitious French operation of the war.

Joffre's plan was to hurl four French armies into an assault against the German lines in Champagne. Pétain's Second Army and Gen. Fernand de Langle de Cary's Fourth Army would deliver the main blows. After these two forces had broken through the German lines, the French Third Army, on the right flank of the main assault, and the French Fifth Army, on the left flank, would join the offensive to add momentum to the attack and further widen the breach in the enemy's defenses. The ultimate objective was nothing less than a complete rupture of the German trench system in northeastern France. This was to be rapidly exploited by a powerful reserve that included many cavalry divisions. Joffre believed that in a matter of a few days' fighting he would push the Germans out of their trenches and transform the campaign in the west from a titanic attritional siege to a decisive battle of maneuver in the open that would decide the war.

The German defenses in Champagne were pounded by artillery fire for three days, and then on September 25, 1915, the French Fourth and Second armies went forward. Facing unexpectedly tough resistance, the Fourth Army's attack quickly bogged down. However, Pétain's Second Army made good progress, and within forty-eight hours his assault divisions had overrun the trench lines of the primary German belt of fortifications. Yet after this initial success he found his troops facing a second fortified sector that was as deep and even more strongly held than the first. What was worse, the French guns had not touched this defensive system. As the Fourth Army struggled to reach its objectives on his left flank amid a rising tide of casualties, Pétain halted his army's attacks and told Joffre that he would need to prepare an assault just as meticulous and just as detailed, with similar amounts of artillery support, to crack the new line of trenches he was facing.

Joffre was frustrated by the attacks' uneven results and attempted to force the situation by feeding in divisions from the strategic reserve that were supposed to be withheld for use in the battle of maneuver once the breakthrough had been made. He also released more of his rapidly dwindling supply of artillery shells to his artillery batteries. With these fresh reinforcements in hand, Pétain and de Cary renewed their attacks but achieved only minimal gains. Meanwhile, the supporting attacks by the flanking Third and Fifth armies were conducted halfheartedly and failed to make any impression on the German defenses. In fairness these armies had planned to exploit a breach rather than make one, but their failures added to the general defeat along the whole line. The battle once more turned into a hopeless frontal assault against a strongly entrenched enemy. Artillery support for the offensive dwindled daily as the batteries swiftly burned through their ammunition stockpiles. A bitterly disappointed Joffre called off the attack on October 7, 1915, and suspended offensive operations for the rest of the year.

Joffre's offensives along the Western Front had failed to make any substantial gains, and there was little to show for the French army's Herculean efforts. The year 1915 was the bloodiest in France's history as more than one million French soldiers were killed, wounded, or missing in the campaigns. Few French commanders had won fame in that vast sea of bloodletting, but Pétain certainly had. In a dizzying ascent, Pétain had risen from a lieutenant colonel in command of an infantry brigade to a general in command of an entire army. He had routinely outperformed his peers at every level of command and seemed destined for great things. Yet although personally successful, Pétain was depressed by the massive defeat suffered in the Champagne battle and believed that Joffre needed to completely revise his thinking on how to conduct the war.

On November 1, 1915, Pétain urged a new approach to this new type of war. He argued that the German army should be worn down through attrition brought about by artillery and not massed infantry assaults and recommended a massive effort on the part of French industry to produce the heavy artillery and munitions required to implement the new strategy. This would have to be accomplished over a period of years, and only then could the French army hope to achieve the type of breakthrough that Joffre envisioned. Pétain told Joffre, "We should not

be afraid to face our difficulties, as we cannot overcome them by deny-
ing their existence."[4]

Joffre dismissed Pétain's ideas as too passive and instead began planning for a new offensive to be launched with the British along the Somme.
He did not include Pétain's Second Army in these plans, possibly because he did not believe Pétain exuded the proper offensive spirit. Joffre
placed the Second Army in strategic reserve for the winter, and Pétain
was happy to have some rest and the opportunity to refit his battered
divisions. Yet even as the final days of December went by uneventfully,
forces were already in motion that would once more place Pétain at the
war's epicenter. His destiny, as well as that of the French army and the
nation they served, would be determined in the coming year at the ancient fortress city of Verdun.

The Victor of Verdun, 1916

As 1915 came to an end, a relative calm settled over the Western Front and Pétain and his Second Army took a well-earned rest. Although winter brought an end to active campaigning, it signaled the start of intensive activity in the Allied high command as General Joffre and his new British counterpart Gen. Douglas Haig began planning an Anglo-French offensive along the Somme River. Joffre and Haig hoped to combine their armies' efforts with near simultaneous offensives by the Russians on the Eastern Front and the Italians along the Isonzo. The concept was to strike the Central Powers in a massive concentric offensive across every front so that, unable to shift forces from one hard-pressed sector to the next to meet the crisis, they would be overwhelmed and defeated.

The chief of the German General Staff, General Falkenhayn, was busy in December 1915 as well, and over the Christmas holiday he submitted a report to Kaiser Wilhelm II regarding Germany's strategic situation in the war. Falkenhayn believed Russia was already on its last legs and would soon collapse. He therefore desired to strike a blow in early 1916 on the Western Front, which he believed to be the most critical theater of war. There Germany faced the two adversaries whom

Falkenhayn deemed the most dangerous—France and Britain. Of these two allies Falkenhayn considered France to be the most vulnerable because the battles of 1915 had pushed the French army to the breaking point. He decided to open a battle in which all the advantages of position and logistics would heavily favor the Germans. To lure the French army to accept battle under such inherently poor terms, Falkenhayn decided to target "objectives for the retention of which the French General Staff would be compelled to throw in every man they have. If they do so the forces of France will bleed to death. . . . If they do not do so, and we reach our objectives, the moral effect on France will be enormous."[1] Of all the potential objectives, Falkenhayn deemed the fortress city of Verdun as the one whose capture could have the most devastating consequences for French morale.

The Romans had been the first to fortify Verdun, and for two thousand years the city had been a bulwark against invasion from the east. The city's heroic resistance during the Franco-Prussian War, during which it had been one of the last major fortresses to surrender to the German invaders, was legendary. After 1871 Verdun became the centerpiece of a massive military engineering project the Third Republic undertook to cauterize France's torn frontiers in the wake of her defeat. A circle of forts was constructed around the city with Fort Douaumont, the largest and most powerful of all, situated on the highest point of ground east of the Meuse River.[2]

The *Région Fortifiée de Verdun* (RFV), as the Verdun sector became designated during the Great War, saw only limited fighting during the 1914 campaign. In fact the German invasion forces had focused their efforts to the north through Belgium, in part because of the formidable fortifications at Verdun. The following year small-scale attacks by both sides and artillery duels occurred in the sector, but again the main battles were elsewhere. The quiet nature of the sector prompted General Joffre to strip the Verdun forts of most of their artillery for use in his offensives in Artois and Champagne during 1915. While practical at a certain level, Joffre's decision rendered the forts, and Verdun, quite vulnerable.

The weakness of Verdun's fortresses did not raise much concern at GQG because by this time the French army believed that the prewar forts were essentially worthless "shell traps," which attracted enemy fire but offered no real shelter from it. This conclusion was based on the German army's swift destruction of the Belgian forts at Liège and the French fortifications at Longwy during the 1914 campaign. However, those forts were constructed of masonry, unlike the Verdun forts, which were made from poured concrete with steel reinforcements. As much as eighteen feet of earth was placed across the reinforcements to cushion the forts from artillery fire. Properly manned and equipped, the forts were formidable defensive positions as would be proved during the battle to come.[3]

Falkenhayn dubbed his Verdun offensive Operation *Gericht*, meaning "place of judgment," or in an arcane usage, "place of execution." The operation entailed the largest concentration of artillery yet used by the Germans, firing in support of an offensive by Crown Prince Wilhelm's German Fifth Army, which would break through the belt of fortresses and capture Verdun. The Germans would then assume strong defensive positions from which they could destroy the inevitable French counter-offensives and, with their overwhelming superiority in artillery, turn Verdun into a slaughter pen for the French army.

On February 21, 1916, more than 3,500 German artillery pieces began to pound the French RFV defenses. After thirty-six hours of this deluge of fire, steel, and poison gas, German infantry began to move forward, expecting only token resistance from the shattered defenders. Instead, small bands of French infantry that had miraculously survived the pounding rose up out of the ground like ghosts. Deafened by explosions and choked by gas, with their trenches caved in, these heroic soldiers fought with the desperation of condemned men. Initially stunned by this fanatical resistance, the Germans recovered and brought forward their special assault teams equipped with flamethrowers, a new weapon designed for use in the Verdun operation. French soldiers barricaded in their collapsed dugouts were burned alive, and thus the isolated pockets of resistance were methodically eradicated.

The French artillery was slow to rise to the challenge, and its barrages were sporadic and uncoordinated. The French 75 mm guns, the most prevalent artillery piece in the sector, lacked the range and firepower to duel the German heavy guns and howitzers, and German counterbattery fire soon made short work of its opposition. Within forty-eight hours of the opening of the attack, French guns on the east bank of the Meuse had been effectively silenced. As French defenses crumbled, Gen. Frédéric Herr, commanding general of the RFV, ordered a tactical withdrawal from the exposed Woëvre Plain so that he could concentrate his forces along the ridgeline east of the city. Herr contemplated a complete abandonment of the east bank of the Meuse before Joffre sent orders that no further withdrawals should be undertaken without his approval. Joffre informed Herr that reinforcements were on the way, and on the night of February 24 he ordered Pétain's Second Army to the threatened sector.

Pétain reported to General Joffre's headquarters at Chantilly on the morning of February 25, 1916. The meeting between the two men was brief. Joffre elaborated on his earlier instructions by ordering Pétain to take command of all forces assembling on the west bank of the Meuse and attach them to his Second Army for the battle's duration. For the time being the Second Army would be subordinated to General Herr's command, but Joffre added, that was subject to change.

Pétain climbed into an open-topped command car for his journey to the battlefield through a foul winter storm. After a full day of driving, Pétain at last arrived at the small town of Souilly around 6:30 p.m. on the night of February 25. The town was approximately fifteen kilometers south of Verdun, astride the main road to the fortress city, and Pétain had chosen to place the Second Army headquarters there. On arriving he was greeted by Joffre's "eyes and ears," Gen. Nöel de Castelnau, who had been sent earlier by Joffre to reconnoiter the situation. Castelnau had been there a short while and could provide Pétain with only sketchy reports on the progress of the fighting that day. Unsatisfied with this information, Pétain decided to journey on to General Herr's headquarters at Dugny to assess the situation himself. As he traveled closer to the battle zone, he found a chaotic situation. The thoroughfare was jammed with ambulances bearing wounded soldiers away from the battle, refugees fleeing the fighting, and his own fresh divisions desperately struggling to move forward.

At length Pétain arrived at Herr's headquarters and entered on a scene of confused desolation. The air was heavy with defeat as bewildered officers, apparently overcome by the magnitude of the events that had befallen them in the past few days, shuffled aimlessly about. Pétain learned from a stricken Herr that Fort Douaumont had fallen to the Germans earlier that day. The Germans had easily repulsed Herr's hastily organized counterattacks, and the fort was now firmly in German hands, making them the masters of the Meuse's east bank. As a consequence, Herr stated, he had ordered all of the forts still in French hands on the east bank to be rigged for demolition in preparation for a general westward withdrawal across the Meuse.

Pétain returned to Souilly at approximately 11:00 p.m. and informed Castelnau of Herr's plans to abandon the right bank and retreat west of the Meuse. Castelnau flew into a fury. Herr's plan was a violation of Joffre's specific orders prohibiting any unauthorized withdrawals. Castelnau said that he had already consulted Joffre on the matter of command in this sector and that they were in agreement that Herr had to go. He produced a small notebook from his pocket and wrote out a terse order in Joffre's name placing Pétain in command of all French forces in the RFV as of midnight. The battle for Verdun was now in the general's hands.

Pétain had little time to ponder the immensity of the task before him. Although he had not slept in the last twenty-four hours, he ignored requests from his staff that he get some rest and instead went to the Souilly town hall, which he had requisitioned from the mayor to serve as his headquarters. As his aides bustled about him, transforming the building into a command post, he began to phone the RFV corps headquarters from his new communications center. To each commanding general he gave the same message: "This is General Pétain speaking. I am taking over command. Inform your troops. Keep up your courage. I know I can depend on you."[4]

He then had his staff place a large-scale map of the Verdun sector on the wall of his new office. Studying the map Pétain realized the east bank of the Meuse allowed precious little room for his forces to maneuver. Yet much of the ridgeline east of Verdun remained in French hands, and he therefore determined, in spite of the loss of Fort Douaumont, to make this position his main line of resistance. Meanwhile, he deployed the bulk of his artillery on the heights west of the Meuse. The guns would be relatively safe there, and the French gunners would be able to pour fire down on the attacking Germans from the commanding hills. Pétain marked out defensive positions for each corps in the RFV, sketched out areas of deployment for reinforcements that were scheduled to arrive over the next few days, and then just before dawn collapsed on a small cot in his new headquarters.

Pétain awakened the next day, February 26, with a high fever and a ferocious cough. His staff summoned a local physician to examine the general, and the doctor diagnosed him as suffering from double pneumonia. The doctor said that at Pétain's age (he was sixty) the illness could be fatal if not treated properly. He prescribed various medications and recommended hospitalization, telling Pétain it was imperative that he rest for at least a week before resuming his duties. Pétain shrugged off the doctor's dire warnings and instead quaffed down the prescribed potions, as well as a variety of his own home remedies, and then went to work. He wrapped a blanket around his fever-wracked body and put on large wool socks that covered his legs from his ankles to his knees, instead of the standard-issue leggings, to help keep warm. He then placed a pot-bellied stove next to his cot along with a small writing desk. From there, perched on the edge of his sickbed, hovering at death's door, Pétain commanded French military operations at Verdun.

Under his able direction the French defenders began to regain their footing and fought back savagely against the surprised Germans, who had thought they had already won the battle. Although Fort Douaumont had fallen, all of the other fortresses in the sector remained in French hands. Pétain countermanded Herr's earlier instructions to demolish these forts and ordered that instead they be reinforced and resupplied. The forts were to become the main centers of resistance on which his defensive line would be based. Although still heavily outgunned and outnumbered, the French doggedly clung to their forts and defensive works along the east bank and repulsed numerous German assaults. Within a few days the German offensive began to lose its momentum, and as the front stabilized the French still held strong positions on the Meuse's east bank.

With the immediate crisis resolved, Pétain focused his attention on his forces' precarious supply situation at Verdun. Prior to the war there had been two major rail lines into Verdun. However, the Germans had cut one in 1914 when they captured the town of Saint-Mihiel, southeast of Verdun. The northern line remained intact, but for the final fifty kilometers into Verdun, it ran precariously close to the German front line and thus was easily interdicted by enemy fire. This left the nearest usable railhead at Bar-le-Duc, some seventy-five kilometers due south of Verdun, and tenuously connected to the fortress city by a light, narrow-gauge railway and a twenty-foot-wide dirt road.

Pétain was able to use the narrow-gauge railway (nicknamed *le Meusien*) to transport some food and fodder for the Second Army, but it was incapable of transporting much of anything else. He immediately ordered a proper rail line to be constructed to Verdun but knew this would take months. Until the rail line was completed his reinforcements, replacements, and ammunition would have to be transported from the railhead at Bar-le-Duc to Verdun. To move the supplies, Pétain utilized the *Service automobile de l'armée française* in the largest use of motorized vehicles seen in warfare to that time. He split the road from Bar-le-Duc to Verdun into six sections. Each section had its own commanding officer and contingent of military police to direct traffic as well as repair shops and refueling stations. The motorized supply convoys were set up to run like trains, administered by the Service automobile and the specially created Traffic Commission of Bar-le-Duc, which together would eventually number 9,000 officers and men with 3,900 vehicles. This force was responsible not only for moving reinforcements to the RFV but also for evacuating wounded and supplying the ammunition needs for a force that eventually numbered more than 500,000 troops. The road from Bar-le-Duc to Verdun was the French army's lifeline during the battle and became known as *La Voie Sacrée*, the "Sacred Way."

In the midst of Pétain's work to organize his supply route the frigid temperatures that had dominated the first days of the battle unexpectedly rose. The newly moderate weather transformed La Voie Sacrée into an impassable morass, and French supply columns ground to an abrupt halt in a river of mud. Pétain met this new challenge by conscripting the townspeople who lived along the road into labor battalions. He established a number of rock quarries and set up relay teams to move the gravel they produced to sites along the road. Work crews of colonial troops from Africa and Asia labored feverishly to shovel the gravel into the mud and firm up the road. The Herculean efforts of these improvised construction battalions allowed trucks to once more roll toward Verdun.

The motorized convoys ran twenty-four hours a day, moving men and matériel to the battle zone. The performance of the Service automobile in the critical opening stages of the Battle of Verdun was nothing short of miraculous. From February 22 to March 8, 1916, French trucks carried 190,000 men, 22,500 tons of munitions, and 2,500 tons of various other materials up La Voie Sacrée to Verdun. Given the ferocity of the German attack, the terrible weather, and the primitive vehicles then in use, it was an amazing achievement.

With his logistical lifeline constructed, Pétain made establishing French fire supremacy on the battlefield his top priority. Pétain later recalled, "I unremittingly urged the activity of the artillery. When the liaison officers of the various army corps, meeting at Souilly for their daily report, began to explain to me in detail the course of fighting on their several fronts, I never failed to interrupt them with the question: 'What have your batteries been doing? We will discuss other points later.'"[5]

On March 19, 1916, Pétain issued a directive to the Second Army that specified that artillery fires be concentrated and ordered artillery observers to use a new report form that would detail the type and objectives of each barrage, the types of projectiles used, the enemy batteries spotted that were vulnerable to counterbattery fire, and other general observations on the effect of the fire. Pétain used these daily reports to direct and coordinate the fire of every battery in the Second Army, a truly monumental task given the incredible number and variety of artillery pieces that Pétain had at his disposal. Pétain concentrated all French artillery batteries under his personal direction and then welded them together into a sledgehammer that he could use when and where he chose. Pétain literally fought fire with fire as his guns unleashed a torrent of steel and flame that made the Germans bleed for every foot of ground they occupied in the Verdun sector. Falkenhayn's plan had relied on the French to counterattack his German forces under their old doctrine of the offensive à outrance, but instead his soldiers faced the fire of Pétain's artillery that inflicted grievous losses on the Germans and made the battlefield of Verdun as much a "place of execution" for the Germans as for the French.

Military aviation came into its own during the Battle of Verdun as it was the first campaign in which the establishment and maintenance of aerial supremacy was a major consideration in the military planning of both sides. The primary missions for aircraft were reconnaissance and artillery spotting. Aircraft and observation balloons were the eyes of the artillery, and throughout the battle, information obtained and passed down from them directed the massive barrages that dominated the Verdun battlefield. The Germans had established air superiority in the battle's early stages, thanks in large part to their Fokker E-III fighter, which was fast and nimble and featured a forward-firing synchronized machine gun. In combination these attributes made it the most lethal fighter plane in the skies in early 1916 and led to the so-called Fokker scourge on the Western Front. German aerial superiority played a significant role in the devastating casualties suffered by French infantry to German artillery fire in the Battle of Verdun's opening stages.

Pétain was one of the first commanders on either side to fully grasp the critical role the airplane had assumed on the modern battlefield. Therefore, on assuming command of the Verdun sector, Pétain made the establishment and maintenance of French aerial supremacy a top priority. To accomplish this, he summoned the pioneering French fighter pilot Comdt. Charles Tricornot de Rose to his headquarters and exclaimed, "Rose, clean the skies for me! I am blind!"[6]

In the weeks that followed, Rose, the "father of French fighters," assembled the best pilots of the *Aéronautique Militaire* to drive the Germans from the skies over Verdun. Rose formed *escadrons de chasse* with these pilots, marking the first time in aviation history that true fighter squadrons had been organized. He eventually formed and coordinated the actions of fifteen such squadrons, including the famed *Escadrille Américaine* (later rechristened the *Escadrille Lafayette*), composed of volunteer American pilots whose first combat experience occurred in the skies over Verdun.

The new French fighter squadrons were originally equipped with the Morane-Saulnier "Bullet," a monoplane that had been used in aerial racing prior to the war. In the spring of 1916, however, the squadrons were upgraded with the Nieuport-11 *Bébé,* a biplane that had been designed as a pure fighter aircraft. Equipped with a forward-firing machine gun for air-to-air combat and aerial rockets to attack observation balloons, the Nieuport-11 was fast, was agile, and proved to be a match for the Fokker E-III, which was its chief rival in the opening stages of the Battle of Verdun. Military aviation progressed so rapidly and the Battle of Verdun lasted so long that both sides further upgraded their squadrons with a whole new generation of fighters over the course of the fighting. By the autumn of 1916, the French were using the Nieuport XVII and the SPAD-VII as their main fighters while by the end of the battle the Germans had introduced the Albatross D-III.

French fighter squadrons began to score numerous victories, and at Pétain's urging, their numbers increased dramatically over the course of the battle. Although Rose was killed in an aerial accident in May, his legacy lived on, and by the summer of 1916 the French had permanently wrested control of the skies over Verdun away from the Germans. The supremacy of the *Aéronautique Militaire* allowed French observation aircraft and tethered balloons to remain almost constantly aloft. French aerial supremacy provided Pétain with intelligence on enemy movements and the French artillery barrages with fire direction, which made the artillery vastly more lethal. Pétain's ability to incorporate the new technology and pioneering tactics of military aviation into his operations at Verdun was a key component to the ultimate French victory in the battle.

In March the Germans shifted the focus of their attack. Suffering heavily from the galling fire of Pétain's guns on the Meuse heights, Crown Prince Wilhelm launched an attack along the Meuse's left bank. French observation aircraft detected the buildup early and Pétain was quick to recognize the threat. He swiftly reinforced the threatened sector with men and guns from his preciously hoarded stockpile of reserves. Thus, by the time the Germans had begun their preliminary bombardment to support their new offensive, Pétain had amassed six divisions on commanding ground, dominated by the ridge known as *Le Mort Homme* and Côte 304. Even with these reinforcements, however, the French line sagged dangerously under the German pounding. Le Mort Homme and Côte 304 briefly fell into German hands and had to be retaken by the French at bayonet point in vicious counterattacks. After further German attacks were stymied in April 1916, the front line stabilized on both banks of the Meuse, and for the first time since assuming command of the sector, Pétain began to feel confident that he would be able to hold Verdun.

The Battle of Verdun settled into a grim struggle of attrition in which the French were at a decided disadvantage. Crammed into a small bridgehead on the river's east bank, they were ringed by German guns that were both more numerous and larger in caliber than their own. Fort Douaumont's fall meant the Germans held the high ground, and the French struggled in a literally uphill fight against their enemy. Yet even under these trying conditions, the French held, and the German offensive ground to a halt. The only advantages the French had were their forts, which at Pétain's insistence were rearmed and transformed from nearly abandoned works into formidable centers of resistance.

The Citadel of Verdun, originally built by Vauban in the seventeenth century and later modernized and reinforced by Raymond Aldophe Séré de Rivières, served as the command post in Verdun itself. Its massive earth-covered walls and roof and subterranean galleries made it an ideal headquarters, hospital, and supply depot. Even the heaviest German guns made little impression on its venerable walls. The main tactical command center for French operations on the Meuse's east bank was Fort Souville, which was one of the more modern forts in the sector. Fort Souville was well built and possessed multiple steel-reinforced concrete machine-gun positions, which rose hydra-like about the underground fortress and spat fire at any who dared approach. This fortress withstood numerous attacks and barred every attempt by the Germans to descend their ridgeline and take Verdun itself. Even the older fortresses proved useful as shelter for reserve formations and as secure areas for stockpiling munitions and supplies.

One of Pétain's best qualities as a commander, which separated him from virtually every other high-ranking officer of World War I, was his sincere concern for the psychological well-being of his men. Pétain wrote,

Indeed my heart bled when I saw our young men of twenty going under fire at Verdun, knowing as I did that with the impressionability of their age they would quickly lose the enthusiasm aroused by their first battle and sink into the apathy of suffering, perhaps even into discouragement, in the face of such a task as theirs. I singled them out for my most affectionate consideration as they moved up into the line with their units. I loved the confident glance with which they saluted me. But the discouragement with which they returned! Their eyes stared into space as if transfixed by a vision of terror. Horrible memories made them quail. When I questioned them, they scarcely answered, and the jeering tones of the old poilus awakened no spark of response in them.[7]

Pétain understood what a tremendous sacrifice was being asked of the soldiers he sent into the line at Verdun and also realized that he could not allow them to be destroyed physically or emotionally in the fighting—or France would have no army left. Pétain therefore instituted a rotational system whereby after approximately three days at the front a division would be withdrawn from Verdun for a week to a quiet area, where it would be allowed to recover from the fighting. The division would then be moved into a more active sector for a few days and then be sent once more into battle at Verdun. Pétain's system was dubbed the *Noria* (roughly "bucket brigade"), and it kept his divisions from being completely shattered. It also allowed the men just enough respite from the battle to keep themselves physically and psychologically strong for the fight. In stark contrast to Pétain's system, the German practice was to keep divisions on the front line at Verdun indefinitely and only withdraw them when they had been virtually destroyed.

Pétain's rotation system was criticized by General Joffre, who in spite of Verdun continued to press forward with his plan to join the British in an offensive along the Somme. Joffre had promised the British that he would provide forty divisions for the forthcoming Somme offensive, but the manpower needs imposed on the French army by the Battle of Verdun and Pétain's use of reserves in his rotation system had consumed most of the planned French contribution. These conflicting needs produced considerable friction between Pétain and Joffre.

Joffre argued that the best way to halt the German attack on Verdun was for the French and their British allies to launch their own offensive in a different sector. Joffre believed that Pétain was so obsessed with Verdun that he had lost perspective on the campaign's place in the overall Allied strategy for the war. Pétain, by contrast, was exceedingly frustrated by a high command that did not recognize that the climactic battle of the war had arrived. He believed that neither the French army nor France itself could survive the terrible blow to morale that Verdun's fall would inflict.

By April Joffre had grown increasingly frustrated at Pétain's refusal to launch a full-scale counteroffensive. Pétain argued it was too soon, and his forces needed more time to recover from the defensive battles of the past several months before going over to the attack themselves. Joffre believed Pétain was being too passive and wanted to see more results from the enormous numbers of men and matériel he had reluctantly transferred to the sector. After numerous discussions and with both generals at an impasse, Joffre made a dramatic move.

In April 1916 Joffre promoted Pétain to command the Central Army Group (GAC), which was composed of Pétain's Second Army as well as the French Third, Fourth, and Fifth armies. Joffre named Pétain's aggressive III Corps commander, Gen. Robert Nivelle, as the new commanding general of the Second Army at Verdun. Joffre believed this new command arrangement would be the best of both worlds. Pétain would now have the resources of an entire army group at his disposal to use as he saw fit at Verdun, and it would in turn enable Joffre to staunch the flow of men and supplies to the Second Army and resume stockpiling resources for the Somme offensive. In addition, Joffre believed Nivelle would be more effective in launching the counteroffensive at Verdun that he had been unsuccessfully pressuring Pétain about for weeks.

Soon after this shake-up, the first major French counteroffensive at Verdun was launched, against Pétain's wishes, on May 22, 1916. The attack's main objective was the reconquest of Fort Douaumont, whose commanding position on the Meuse's east bank and political value as a symbol of the German's early success made it a prized objective. Nivelle's attack made good progress at first, but the Germans, as Pétain had feared, were still too strong. Although the assaulting forces actually reached the fortress's superstructure, they were driven off within hours by strong

German counterattacks. Nivelle's attempts to reinforce his early success and renew the attack on the fort only resulted in heavy casualties with little ground gained, and at length Pétain intervened and cancelled the operation.

In the wake of the failed counteroffensive Pétain reasserted his authority over military operations at Verdun. Although in theory the new command structure designed by Joffre had relieved Pétain of his responsibilities at Verdun, which was only one sector of his new command, he resumed overall direction of French operations in the battle and henceforth kept General Nivelle on a short leash.

In June the Germans resumed offensive operations with a powerful attack aimed at capturing Fort Vaux and driving the French forces off the Meuse's east bank. The attack went well at first, and the Germans made good progress, quickly overrunning outlying French positions and then heading toward Fort Vaux. Comdt. Sylvain-Eugène Raynal defended Fort Vaux with a force of approximately six hundred men, which included many wounded soldiers who had sought shelter in the fort as the German offensive swept forward. Fort Vaux was pounded by massive German railway guns and heavy howitzers and then attacked by an entire German corps, led by special assault teams armed with flamethrowers. Yet for almost an entire week Raynal and his gallant force turned aside the German assaults. Raynal and his men resisted flames, shells, and poison gas but succumbed to thirst when their water supplies ran out.[8]

Although Fort Vaux fell, the defensive stand made there wrecked the latest German attack toward Verdun. The engagement proved once more the power of the French fortifications in the RFV. In fact, during the entire ten months of battle, the Germans captured only two forts, Douaumont and Vaux.

By the summer of 1916, the situation on the ground at Verdun began to change. The Franco-British offensive at the Somme on July 1, 1916, placed tremendous demands on the Germans fighting on the Western Front. As a clamor arose for troops and guns to be stripped from his sector to reinforce the Somme, Crown Prince Wilhelm's Fifth Army made one final supreme effort to capture Verdun on July 12,

1916, but after several days of intense combat, this final attack was turned back with heavy losses to the Crown Prince's forces and General Falkenhayn's plan to capture Verdun now lay wrecked.

The Germans' failure to capture Verdun had dramatic repercussions for the German army. In August 1916 the kaiser relieved General Falkenhayn as chief of the General Staff and replaced him with FM Paul von Hindenburg, who, along with his brilliant chief of staff Gen. Erich Ludendorff, had achieved a series of great victories over the Russians on the Eastern Front. Shortly after assuming their new positions, Hindenburg and Ludendorff toured the Western Front, with which they were unfamiliar. The grueling siege warfare waged there in no way resembled the sweeping war of movement across open plains they had fought on the Eastern Front.

The grim battlefield of Verdun shocked Hindenburg and Ludendorff. Hindenburg described Verdun as "a regular hell" and informed Kaiser Wilhelm II that "the battles there exhaust our army like an open wound." He believed that victory was no longer possible at Verdun and ordered an immediate halt to all offensive operations at Verdun. He followed this up with a directive in September 1916 instructing Crown Prince Wilhelm that the positions now held should be consolidated into permanent defensive positions. As far as the German high command was concerned the Battle of Verdun was over, and it was Hindenburg's great hope that the French would allow the battle to end there. The French, however, did not intend to accept the status quo.

Throughout August 1916 General Nivelle and Gen. Charles Mangin carried out a number of small-scale attacks at Verdun that produced solid, if unspectacular, gains. These modest successes prompted them to plan for further such attacks in September, but Pétain overruled them. He preferred instead to prepare a large-scale operation that could have potentially decisive results on the battlefield. However, this meant carefully stockpiling men, guns, and ammunition for about a month to build up a force capable of undertaking the operation he envisioned. Nivelle and Mangin protested the shackling of their pinprick attacks, stating that they needed to remain aggressive to retain initiative on the battlefield, but Pétain eventually won them over to his plan for a large-scale operation.[9]

With the city safely in French hands and German strength and ambition waning dramatically in this sector of the front, it was decided to make a formal gesture to imbue Verdun as a symbol of French defiance to the invader. With this in mind, on September 12, 1916, French president Raymond Poincaré, along with Joffre, Pétain, and numerous other generals, politicians, and foreign dignitaries, gathered at Verdun to award the city the Légion d'honneur in recognition of its heroic defense. Pétain was quiet during the celebration as he believed the festivities were premature. While a defensive victory had indeed been won, Pétain believed the victory could not be complete until Fort Douaumont was once more in French hands.

On September 20, 1916, Pétain sent Joffre a plan for a major counteroffensive at Verdun. Pétain's ambitious attack was designed to recapture Fort Douaumont, as well as Fort Vaux, and drive the Germans off the commanding high ground east of the Meuse. Knowing his chief to be obsessed with the battle raging along the Somme, Pétain pointed out that his proposed attack could provide much needed support to British and French forces bogged down in their battle to the north by drawing German attention and resources back to Verdun. Joffre was pleased with Pétain's aggressive scheme and swiftly approved the operation.

Pétain chose General Mangin to lead the attack, which would be composed of three assault divisions, three supporting divisions, and one division in general reserve, collectively known as *Groupement Mangin*. The seven divisions slated for the attack were brought up to full strength with replacements from the training depots that mainly consisted of new recruits from the class of 1916. The veterans provided a solid nucleus, and the rebuilt divisions were a good mix of combat experience and youthful enthusiasm. The assault battalions were equipped with special weapons, including grenade launchers, automatic rifles, and deadly *lance-flammes* (flamethrowers). Pétain was heavily involved in planning every detail of the attack as well as making plans for the resupply and reinforcement of the assault troops so that they would be able to hold the ground they won.

On October 19, 1916, the French preliminary bombardment began. Observation balloons went up all along the French lines before Douaumont and French observation planes soared aloft to direct the deadly fire of approximately seven hundred heavy artillery pieces on the German positions. As German fighters rose to meet these intruders, French pursuit squadrons, many equipped with the rugged new SPAD-VII fighter, inflicted heavy losses. Within forty-eight hours the French fighters had essentially driven their enemies from the skies and established aerial supremacy over the battlefield. With unfettered observation of the battlefield French guns rained down a deadly accurate artillery fire, which began to systematically smash the German defenses.

As the bombardment increased in volume the French unveiled their new 400 mm railway guns, the heaviest artillery yet employed on the battlefield by the French army. The target for the new "super-heavy" guns was Fort Douaumont, which they began to methodically hammer with a precision that severely rattled the nerves of the German defenders sheltering within its mighty walls.

On October 21 the French barrage abruptly halted, and the fires of the heavy guns shifted to pounding reserve trenches and assembly areas while a curtain of bursting steel dropped just in front of the French lines and began creeping toward the German trenches at regularly timed intervals. All along the line, French infantry opened up with rifles and automatic weapons and French battle cries pierced the air. German defenders hastily scrambled from their underground bunkers to man their fighting positions along the front line while signal rockets went up to summon their artillery batteries into action, most of which had remained concealed throughout the duration of the French preparatory barrages. The German guns were now unmasked and began shooting their preregistered fires in a deluge of high explosives designed to decimate the French assault waves. However, the shells struck nothing but ground.

The entire "attack" had been a ruse, designed by Pétain and Nivelle to lure the German infantry out of their protective bunkers and tempt the concealed German batteries into firing and revealing their positions. French aircraft spotted the enemy guns, noted their locations, and then provided fire direction for the long-range French 155 mm guns as they cut loose with a deadly accurate counterbattery fire on the German guns. Simultaneously, heavy French guns began to pound the main German defense line, which was now packed with enemy infantry. The guns viciously hammered the exposed defenders, who suffered grievous losses before regaining the shelter of their dugouts. The counterbattery fire was also extremely effective, and over the course of the next three days more than half of the German artillery batteries within range of Douaumont were destroyed. French artillery kept up a methodical pounding of the German defenses, and by the night of October 23 their barrages had inflicted severe damage and established near absolute fire supremacy over the battlefield.[10]

On October 24, 1916, General Joffre traveled to Verdun to be present when the attack went in and, he hoped, to share in the glory of the triumph. To keep the Germans off balance the French eschewed the traditional dawn starting time of an offensive. Instead they lulled the Germans into a false sense of security by remaining inactive during the morning hours. They unexpectedly attacked on the afternoon of October 24. Mangin's troops went forward with an enthusiasm that had not been seen on the Verdun battlefield for some time; it was as if they sensed that this attack would be different. German defenses began to crumble right away, and the lead assault battalions of Groupement Mangin were soon advancing on the looming eminence of Fort Douaumont. As they swarmed toward the formidable position, they caught the German defenders off guard. One of the 400 mm railway shells had penetrated the fort and started a fire that forced a temporary evacuation of the fortress. The fire was brought under control, but the French infantry caught the Germans in the open before they could resume their positions in the fort and wiped them out. Signal rockets rose over Fort Douaumont while mirrors were used to flash a single message back to the tactical command post at Fort Souville: *Victoire*. Cheers resounded through the French high command as the realization set in that after eight agonizing months, Fort Douaumont was back in French hands. General Joffre shared in the jubilation and later recalled, "That day of October 24th was the happiest I spent during the entire war. . . . The victory . . . completed the defeat of the Germans before Verdun."[11]

The attack was not yet over, however. After a series of unsuccessful counterattacks, the German line began to give way throughout the entire Douaumont sector of the Verdun front. Steady advances were made throughout the week that threatened to encircle and annihilate large numbers of German troops. Crown Prince Wilhelm was forced to abandon Fort Vaux, his other great prize, and make a tactical withdrawal off the dominant ridgeline east of the Meuse that his forces had captured early in the battle. Indeed, all of the German successes to this point at Verdun had come undone. Ludendorff later lamented, "The French attacked on the 24th; we lost Fort Douaumont, and on November 1 were obliged to evacuate Fort Vaux also. The loss was grievous, but still more grievous was the totally unexpected decimation of some of our divisions."[12]

German losses during the French counteroffensive of October were severe, even by World War I standards. In just three days of battle the French inflicted 20,000 casualties on the Germans and captured 15 artillery pieces, including 5 heavy guns, 51 *minenwerfers*, and 144 machine guns. The French official history later appropriately termed the triumph *La Belle Victoire*.[13]

Still Pétain was not satisfied. After consolidating his positions atop Douaumont, he decided that the Germans needed to be pushed farther back to make sure the fortress would not be in danger of any sudden enemy counterattack. Therefore, he prepared a final coup de grâce for the Germans. On December 15, 1916, the French attacked once more. Again they focused the full might of their guns and infantry on precise objectives and closely coordinated their artillery barrages to support the advancing infantry. The result was another French success, and as the Battle of Verdun drew to a close in the midst of a snowstorm on December 16, 1916, the Germans had been essentially pushed all the way back to their original starting positions of February. This final attack sealed the French victory at Verdun and dealt a heavy blow to the Germans. Ludendorff later wrote, "We not only suffered heavy casualties, but also lost important positions. The strain during this year had proved too great. The endurance of the troops had been weakened by long spells of defense under the powerful enemy artillery fire and their own losses. We were completely exhausted on the Western Front."[14]

The Battle of Verdun, one of the longest and bloodiest in history, was immediately hailed by contemporaries in France and elsewhere as "the greatest battle in her thousand years of military history."[15] Coming as it did in a year of heavy Allied defeats in Russia, Italy, the Balkans, and at the Somme, the French triumph at Verdun shone like a lone beacon in a dark sea of despair. At the start of the year Germany was in a dominant position and stood poised to win the Great War. Yet in spite of achieving numerous victories, the German failure at Verdun denied them the strategic success they longed for and ensured that the war would go on and France would survive.

The victory had been dearly bought and many had contributed to the triumph, including Nivelle and Mangin, who were heaped with praise by the press and government. Yet above them all towered Pétain. In spite of their sometimes heated differences, General Joffre was among the first to proclaim Pétain the "Victor of Verdun" and later wrote, "What saved Verdun was [Pétain's] highly developed tactical sense, his continual perfecting of the methods of defense, and the constant improvement he effected in the organization of the command of the higher units. General Pétain was the heart and soul of the action."[16]

Commander in Chief of the French Army, 1917–1918

After the failure of the Somme offensive and revelations of his poor preparations for the defense of Verdun, the French government relieved Joffre of his position as commander in chief of the French army in December 1916. Joffre's natural successor appeared to be Pétain as the soldiers of the French army saw him as their champion and he had emerged from Verdun as the greatest French commander of the war. However, the French government did not share this high opinion of Pétain. Pétain disdained politicians and made little attempt to conceal his thoughts. His condescending demeanor served to politically isolate him from most of the influential policymakers in Paris. Therefore, the government chose Gen. Robert Nivelle for the post. Nivelle had worked hard to curry favor with members of the Chamber of Deputies and had won many powerful friends in the government who saw him as a far more acceptable choice as commander.

On assuming command Nivelle announced that he had a "formula for victory" that would break the deadlock on the Western Front and win the war in a single dramatic offensive. He intended to use the "rolling barrage" he had developed at Verdun on a grand scale to support a powerful concentric attack against the German salient in Champagne along the Aisne River and the Chemin des Dames ridge. He believed that his attack would break open the German trench system on the first day of battle. Nivelle promised anxious politicians a swift victory that in a matter of weeks would hurl the German invaders back to the Rhine and liberate occupied France.

Unfortunately for France, Nivelle's plan was heavily flawed in that, owing to the operation's massive scale, the French would not be able to provide the same concentration of artillery fire they had achieved during their limited offensives at Verdun in the fall of 1916. Nivelle was also terribly indiscreet and spoke far too freely to the French and foreign press regarding the operation. German intelligence officers easily learned that a major French offensive was in the offing as well as where and when the French would strike.

The Germans responded by constructing the *Siegfriedstellung* behind the front line along the north-central sector of the Western Front. The new German defense system (christened the "Hindenburg Line" by the Allies) implemented everything the Germans had learned in nearly three years of trench warfare. It was a multilayered defensive network of steel-reinforced concrete bunkers and trenches protected by belts of barbed wire hundreds of feet wide with German guns zeroed in on all likely avenues of attack. On the eve of Nivelle's great offensive, the Germans executed a tactical withdrawal out of their salient in Champagne and fell back into these formidable defensive works.

Though Nivelle remained supremely confident in his plan even as the Germans withdrew and reinforced their positions, Pétain and other senior officers charged with carrying out the attack had become skeptical of the prospects for success and decided to go over Nivelle's head and inform French minister of war Paul Painlevé of their concerns. Pétain and Gen. Joseph Micheler, who commanded the Reserve Army Group (GAR), told Painlevé that there was little chance of achieving a breakthrough. They argued that the German withdrawal would force the French to make a frontal assault against strongly held positions. Pétain warned that Nivelle's attempt to achieve a mass breakthrough along a broad sector of the front would lead to a "massacre" and argued for a limited attack with more realistic goals.[1]

In response to these reservations, Premier Alexandre Ribot, President Raymond Poincaré, and Painlevé held a conference with Nivelle and his four army group commanders on April 6, 1917, to discuss the forthcoming attack. At the meeting both Poincaré and Painlevé urged Nivelle to reconsider launching the attack, but in the presence of their commander, the French generals were for the most part hesitant to voice their opinions. Pétain, however, was not afraid to speak up. He stated that he believed the attack was pointless. Even if the French army could achieve a breakthrough, which he thought was highly unlikely, it could not be properly exploited. Pétain asked, "Have we five hundred thousand fresh troops to make an advance? No. Then it is impossible."[2]

Nivelle was infuriated by Pétain's criticism and was further angered by the government and his army group commanders, who remained silent when he asked for their support. The commander in chief abruptly offered to resign, an action the French government apparently was not prepared for. All of France knew about the impending offensive, and it was unthinkable that Nivelle would resign on the eve of the great battle. In fact, the political repercussions from such an event could bring down Ribot's shaky government.

Sensing that his threat to resign had achieved its desired effect, Nivelle became the charmer. He promised that if he were not successful after two days of fighting, he would halt the attack. Pétain was unconvinced, but the French politicians and other army group commanders backed down and Nivelle was granted permission to proceed with his offensive.

After a violent preparatory artillery barrage, the French poilus went over the top on April 16, 1917, in a driving storm of sleet and hurled themselves against the Hindenburg Line and the heavily fortified German positions along the Chemin des Dames. To their dismay the French assault battalions quickly discovered that the initial bombardment had failed to open sufficient gaps in the vast belts of barbed wire. As the troops struggled through the twisted maze of wire entanglements at an agonizingly slow pace, German machine guns and artillery, carefully placed and well protected, began to exact a frightful toll.

Nivelle's "formula" of using rolling artillery barrages to support the infantry quickly broke down as the fires moved forward according to a rigid timetable based on overly optimistic estimates of how much ground the infantry could cover in the initial assault. When the French infantry advance bogged down in the face of heavy German resistance, the poilus watched in dismay as their artillery fire shifted to new targets according to the schedule Nivelle had assigned to them. The infantry was eventually stranded with no artillery support. Foul weather and the resurgent Imperial German air force made aerial observation, which had been critical to coordinating these types of barrages in Nivelle's previous attacks, difficult. In spite of this, the French infantry displayed remarkable élan and tenacity in its attacks and succeeded in clawing out a toehold in the German defenses but at a frightful cost in casualties. As reports of the initial attacks' failure to achieve the anticipated breakthrough filtered in, Nivelle ignored his promise to break off the offensive within forty-eight hours if it were not successful and instead committed wave after wave of infantry to the increasingly futile assaults. Nivelle's badly coordinated attacks achieved only minimal gains for a heavy cost in lives. During the week of April 16–23, 1917, the French army suffered approximately 120,000 casualties.[3]

At length even Nivelle's confidence was shaken, and he sought out the advice and support of his former chief Pétain. On April 27, 1917, Nivelle asked Pétain if he would be willing to join his staff as an adviser, but Pétain curtly refused. He had no intention of joining the staff of an individual whom he had never had confidence in and whose ability to command the French army he seriously questioned. It is also distinctly possible that Pétain, who could clearly see that Nivelle's star was sinking, was already considering the possibility that the French government might ask him to replace Nivelle. Regardless, Nivelle was dismayed by the rebuff and left Pétain's headquarters feeling thoroughly dejected. Nivelle knew no other way to salvage his career than to continue the attack and hope that somehow he could break through the German lines, but events soon overtook him.

By late April 1917 French military intelligence had become increasingly disturbed by the defeatist nature of letters being sent home by French soldiers, many of whom had reached the limits of human endurance. The French army's morale plummeted dangerously and the soldier's confidence in Nivelle disappeared as the battle turned into yet another slugging match with minimal gains for exorbitant casualties.

Pessimism as to the war's outcome and anger at those in charge of the army and government became more and more widespread among the rank and file. Nivelle's offensive had achieved little other than to add to the already prodigious pile of dead poilus, and it was apparent that the French army had reached its breaking point.

On April 29, 1917, a French infantry battalion refused to go back into the line, and then on May 3, 1917, an entire division mutinied en masse when the men learned that they were being sent back to the front instead of to the rest area they had been promised. More units followed suit, and large numbers of French soldiers remained in their trenches and refused to attack. By the time the French government intervened and ordered Nivelle to halt the offensive on May 9, 1917, more than half of the divisions in the army were in various stages of indiscipline and mutiny.[4]

On May 15, 1917, Painlevé took a dramatic step toward rectifying the situation by relieving Gen. Robert Nivelle of command of the French army and replacing him with the hero of the common soldier and a military figure still admired by the French people, Pétain. Painlevé believed that no man but Pétain could win back the soldiers' confidence and rally the army to the defense of the Third Republic, and the Ribot government grudgingly agreed. Charles de Gaulle later wrote, "On the day when France had to choose between ruin and reason, Pétain was promoted."[5]

Pétain made suppression of the mutiny and the recovery of the French army's moral and physical strength his top priorities. Rather than implementing a brutal crackdown, Pétain showed leniency to all but the most hard-core mutineers. He began a remarkable tour of the front lines, speaking to virtually the entire French army, one battalion at a time. Pétain's speeches varied, but for the most part the major themes were repeated at every stop. He told the men that he understood their frustration at the length and cost of the war, but that the army and the nation desperately needed them at this grave hour. The enemy still held France's sacred soil and hundreds of thousands of French people lived under the invader's ironhanded rule. The government and people of France depended on them to be their liberators and their defenders. Pétain also told the soldiers that no more major offensives would be undertaken until their strength had been built up. He told them the future looked bright: tanks were being mass-produced and the Americans were on their way to aid France. He often concluded his talks by saying, "We shall wait for the Americans and the tanks," a statement which invariably brought forth wild cheers and applause from the poilus.[6]

American troops were indeed on their way to Europe, albeit still at a trickle. The first contingent arrived to much fanfare in July 1917. Thanks to a military mission led by Marshal Joffre, the United States decided to place the bulk of the nascent American Expeditionary Force (AEF) under the care and tutelage of the French army. Pétain realized that victory or defeat in the Great War hinged on the Americans, and the importance of the Franco-American relationship was paramount in his mind. As a result Pétain took the training of the AEF and its preparation for a major role on the Western Front as one of his highest priorities. He personally helped select officers to serve as trainers with the AEF and issued numerous instructions to French officers, ordering them to go out of their way to treat American soldiers with respect and with all the deference due the armed representatives of France's sister republic. He also encouraged the French officers to form personal friendships with their American counterparts as a way of establishing a closer working relationship between the two armies.

One offshoot of this policy was the relationship forged between Pétain and AEF commander Gen. John J. Pershing. Both men were professional soldiers, with notoriously gruff demeanors, but instead of acrimony they felt a mutual admiration for one another, which grew into a true friendship. Pershing recognized that Pétain was doing his utmost to build an autonomous American army, even to the point of depleting French stockpiles of precious weapons such as tanks and fighter planes to make the AEF an effective force. Pershing did not initially agree with Pétain's methods, which he found to be too cautious, but he later grew to appreciate the French commander's tactics. In fact, after the war the normally reserved Pershing enthusiastically embraced Pétain before a gathering of senior AEF officers and, with his arm wrapped tightly around his friend, pronounced Pétain to be "the greatest general the war produced."

Throughout the fall of 1917 tens of thousands of raw American soldiers were shipped across the Atlantic and rushed into French training camps, but the war had begun to go terribly badly for the Allies. In November the Bolshevik Revolution toppled Alexander Kerensky's pro-Allied provisional government, plummeting Russia into civil war. Vladimir Lenin's new government entered into peace negotiations with Germany, and while the peace agreement was not formally signed until March 1918, it was clear to everyone that Russia was out of the war. That freed up more than one million German soldiers for service on the Western Front, and for the first time since the war began, the German army's might could be focused on a single theater of operations.

On the Western Front, the French army conducted limited offensives in August and again in October designed by Pétain to provide sound tactical adjustments to his line as well as to restore fighting spirit and confidence in the badly shaken French soldiery. Although the attacks were successful, they were mere pinpricks to the great offensives that had gone before and did little real damage to the Germans. Meanwhile, British FM Sir Douglas Haig's latest offensive, the Third Battle of Ypres, or Passchendaele, began with great promise in July but ended in defeat in November amid a mountain of casualties. The BEF was exhausted, and British prime minister David Lloyd George had lost all faith in Haig. At the Allied Supreme War Council all eyes were fixed on the spring of 1918, when it was expected that the Germans, having rested and refitted their eastern divisions, would unleash a powerful attack on the Western Front that neither the British nor the French high command had great optimism in stopping. To Pétain and many others, the wild card in this situation was the AEF. If the U.S. Army could arrive in sufficient numbers, and if its soldiers could be properly trained and equipped in a timely manner, it could yet turn the tide against Germany and provide the Allies with the numbers of men and matériel necessary for victory. The bulk of this responsibility lay with Pétain and the French army, and in the waning weeks of 1917 the general redoubled his efforts to drill the Americans into a powerful fighting force. At a dinner held for the officers of Pershing and Pétain's staffs in late 1917, the mood was jovial as both sides spoke of women, wine, and victory. In the midst of the reverie Pétain, who had remained glumly silent throughout the evening at last broke into the conversation and, in an ominous tone of voice, said, "I hope it is not too late."

On March 21, 1918, the concentrated fire of more than 6,000 artillery pieces announced the opening of Operation Michael, Imperial Germany's attempt to win the Great War. The Germans struck near the old Somme battlefield and ruptured the British line where the BEF and French army maintained their point of contact, thereby separating the two armies. Within forty-eight hours of brutal fighting the British had lost their battle zone and been driven into the open. British forces fell back toward the channel ports, which were not only their supply source but also their means of evacuation from the continent if the front collapsed. Pétain ordered several divisions north to help the British but directed his main force to fall back toward Paris and used the bulk of his reserves to screen the city and prevent the German offensive from driving south toward the French capital.

As the Allies retreated in two separate directions, the gap between them swung wide open, and Field Marshal Hindenburg and General Ludendorff poured troops through the breach. The greatest crisis since the First Battle of the Marne had arrived, and the outcome of the war and the fate of the world hung in the balance. In this tense climate a critical conference was held at Doullens between the senior officers of the BEF and the French army as well as political representatives from both countries. The crisis was obvious, and if the Germans succeeded in completely separating the two Allies they could defeat each one in detail and win the war. What was needed was a supreme Allied commander to coordinate the movements of both armies as well as that of the Italian army and the nascent formations of the AEF. Given that the bulk of troops on the Western Front were French and that Haig did not have the confidence of his own government, it was assumed that a French general would be chosen for the post. Pétain was the commanding general of the French army, but he had also become a pronounced Anglophobe. He had little respect for Haig and neither liked nor trusted the British, and in addition he was in a darkly pessimistic mood at the conference. At one point, while he was speaking with the new French premier

Georges Clemenceau, Pétain gestured toward Haig and said, "There is a man who will be obliged to capitulate in [the] open field within a fortnight, and [we will be] very lucky if we are not obliged to do the same."[7]

Clemenceau respected Pétain but could abide neither his pessimism nor his disdain for the politicians of the Third Republic. Clemenceau also knew that a supreme Allied commander would have to work closely with the British, which Pétain obviously could not do. As a consequence Clemenceau threw his support behind Gen. Ferdinand Foch. The British enthusiastically supported this nomination, and Pétain found himself passed over once more.

Pétain did not care for Foch's exuberant overconfidence and could not help but recall that Foch had been one of the great prophets of the cult of the offensive that had led to such disaster in 1914. Nevertheless, he had a grudging respect for the man and accepted the appointment with scarcely a murmur of protest. In fact, Pétain did not particularly want the job, which he viewed as more of a political go-between rather than a military office. Although he would be mistaken in that initial assessment, he remained content in his post as commanding general of the French army.

On becoming supreme Allied commander, Foch sent large numbers of French divisions from Pétain's jealously hoarded reserves to reestablish contact with the BEF and take over large sections of the British sector in order to allow Haig to concentrate his forces on a narrower front. British resistance stiffened, and Operation Michael ran out of steam but not before it had grievously damaged the BEF and won a large swath of territory.

General Ludendorff directed the German offensives in 1918, and he yearned to launch a new attack to finish off the British. However, he was dismayed by the large number of French divisions in the north and believed it was first necessary to clear these units out before proceeding. To divert French forces away from the British sector, Ludendorff authorized Operation Blücher, which was designed as a diversionary attack against the French positions along the Chemin des Dames in central France, opposite Paris. A strong blow here, Ludendorff believed, would frighten the French into withdrawing their units from the British sector and thus enable him to launch his final attack to finish off the BEF.

On May 27, 1918, German soldiers went forward and unexpectedly broke clean through the French lines. The French forces had been too bunched up in the front lines, and when their flanks were turned, large numbers were captured and a gaping hole was torn in the French line. As German troops rushed through the opening, Ludendorff abruptly realized that this "diversionary" attack could actually lead to a decisive blow against the French, and therefore he rushed reinforcements in to exploit the breakthrough.

The breakthrough before Paris was just what Pétain had feared most, and he was furious at Foch for having depleted the French strategic reserve to reinforce the British. Pétain took what units he had available and deployed them against of the onrushing Germans, but as one of Pétain's staff officers later recalled, they "disappeared like drops of rain on white hot iron."[8] With the situation becoming more critical by the hour, Foch began shifting divisions south as rapidly as he could, but there could be little help expected from the battered British forces in the north. As June began German forces once more reached the banks of the Marne and the French capital was a scant fifty miles away. The Chamber of Deputies began to contemplate plans for the evacuation of the government, but Premier Clemenceau refused to be moved. He informed the Chamber of Deputies that he had the utmost confidence in the French army's leadership and that there would be no surrender; it was to be a fight to the finish.

At this critical moment General Pershing informed Pétain that the AEF should be deployed to its own sector and take part in the battle. Pétain thanked his friend but pointed out that while there was no questioning the fighting spirit of the Americans, they lacked the essential support units and logistical structure to operate autonomously. Pershing reluctantly admitted that this was indeed the case and then said that he would agree to have AEF units placed under French command for the duration of the crisis. Pétain was thrilled by this news and told Pershing they should go right away and inform Foch, which they did. At Foch's headquarters Pershing issued a formal pronouncement in which he declared, "All that we have is yours, use us as you wish. The American people will be proud to take part in the greatest battle of history."[9]

A number of American divisions were sent to take over a quiet sector in Alsace to free up French units for the battle, while two American units, the Second and Third divisions, were thrown directly into the path of the advancing Germans. Alongside their French allies, the Americans fought the Germans to a standstill at Château-Thierry and Belleau Wood. They then counterattacked and drove the Germans away from the French capital. The crisis had passed, but the AEF was now firmly committed to battle in the French sector. Pétain was thrilled by the performance of the Franco-American forces and believed their success boded well for the future.

In spite of the failure of his tactically brilliant offensives to deliver a strategic defeat to the Allies, Ludendorff remained convinced that victory was within his grasp. He believed that through a series of such tactical victories the war could be won. By July 1918 he thought that the French and British armies were on the verge of falling apart and that their governments would soon lose the will to continue the war. Germany would thereby achieve victory in the Great War before the arrival of more American soldiers could tip the balance of the scales in favor of the Allies.

Ludendorff, however, was running out of time in his race to end the war before the Americans could arrive on the Western Front in strength. When the first German offensive of 1918 had burst across the British lines along the Somme in March there were 300,000 inexperienced American soldiers scattered throughout France. Yet just four months later that number had quadrupled to 1.2 million.[10] Ludendorff recognized that he needed to undertake another offensive and secure a decisive victory before even more Americans entered the battle. To this end, he began planning a major offensive to be undertaken in July by the Army Group of German crown prince Wilhelm against the French and American forces in the Reims salient in Champagne. If successful the attack would destroy large numbers of French troops as well as the cream of the infant AEF and secure a bridgehead south of the Marne River that could be used as a base for an attack on Paris. Ludendorff also hoped that the shock of losing a large number of troops as well as the great city of Reims might be enough to knock France out of the war or at least permanently cripple the French army's offensive capability.

As German forces began to mass for the coming attack, the operation became an open secret and the German press christened the widely rumored forthcoming operation as *Friedenstürm*, or "Peace Offensive." The thought that this would be the final battle of the war inspired the German soldiers as well as civilians on the German home front. Ludendorff too believed that the climactic battle of the war was at hand.

The Allies also thought that a critical juncture in the war had been reached. Foch and Pétain had begun planning a Franco-American offensive against the German forces occupying the Marne salient, but just as they were readying the attack, American and French military intelligence learned of the German plans to attack Reims. Foch's first instinct was to preempt the German attack with his own offensive, but Pétain argued against it. Pétain pointed out that if the Germans struck in Champagne, then they would make themselves even more vulnerable to Foch's blow against their Marne salient. Pétain therefore advised Foch to make his attack a counteroffensive that would catch the Germans off balance and when they were at their most vulnerable, having already committed themselves to the attack. Foch reluctantly agreed and ordered Pétain to prepare for two battles, a defensive battle followed by a counteroffensive.

As Pétain arranged the forces provided to him by Foch, he purposely scattered the American divisions among his French formations to stiffen the defenses of as many sectors of the French line as possible. Without question this was done as much for moral effect as for reasons of military necessity. Pétain reasoned that the more French soldiers saw Americans in the battle, the more the overall morale of the French army would be buoyed by the presence of their allies. The Americans would be fighting side by side with the French in the coming engagement, and Pétain wanted to make sure that as many French soldiers as possible saw that this was the case.[11]

The deployment of the French forces in the Reims salient was modeled on Pétain's tactical doctrine as he had expressed it in December 1917 in his Directive Number 4 to the French army. This order urged that the French army abandon its practice of meeting an enemy offensive by crowding as many men into the front line as possible. Pétain advocated a thinly held front line manned almost exclusively by small teams of machine gunners. The main line of resistance was to be established behind this front line and echeloned in depth. This would ensure that far fewer French soldiers would be exposed to the fury of the preparatory artillery barrage and especially the crushing fire of the short-ranged minenwerfers.

On July 15, 1918, the great German offensive that would become known as the Second Battle of the Marne began. The initial main drive was an attack by the German First and Third armies against the eastern flank of the Reims salient, while the German Seventh Army simultaneously struck the salient's western face. The plan was to achieve a double envelopment of the Franco-American positions at Reims. However, right from the start the battle went badly for the Germans. Allied intelligence deduced the timing of the German attack and just before the scheduled bombardment was to begin, French guns unleashed a powerful barrage of their own. They pounded the densely packed German assault formations, inflicting grievous casualties and badly disrupting the attack. German forces encountered unexpectedly stiff resistance from the French machine-gun teams whose "islands of resistance" proved to be more difficult to overcome than expected. After penetrating the French front-line position, the German infantry was surprised to see how few French soldiers had actually been involved in holding up their advance and were concerned by the apparent lack of casualties caused by their preparatory bombardment.

As the German assault battalions prepared to press forward, they were dismayed to see looming before them an extremely formidable defensive system: the French main line of defense, which had been constructed behind the front line and consequently had been virtually untouched by their artillery barrage. The Germans realized that this new system could never be carried without considerable artillery support, but the new defense line was beyond the range of most of their batteries and thus they would have to laboriously move their artillery and ammunition forward. As they did so, they came under devastating fire from French and American artillery and took heavy losses in the attempt. The German infantry gallantly tried to press the attack even without adequate artillery support but were thrown back by the determined French and American defenders.

Crown Prince Wilhelm was dismayed when he received news of the disastrous defeat suffered by the German First and Third armies before Reims. Although encouraged by the tactical success achieved by the German Seventh Army in crossing the Marne, he believed that the defeat suffered in the east severely compromised the overall chances for the operation's success. The crown prince nevertheless determined to continue the attack even though, as he later wrote, "in my heart of hearts I had to admit the bitter truth that the offensive had failed."[12]

The crown prince held out hope that the Seventh Army could exploit its small success and perhaps make a serious enough penetration across the Marne that the French high command would panic and abandon the exposed Reims salient. With this in mind, Crown Prince Wilhelm ordered a resumption of the offensive the next day with the Seventh Army, while he ordered the First and Third armies to essentially launch only holding attacks to their front.

Pétain was swift to react to the results of the first day's battle. The Germans' crossing of the Marne and their success gained along the western face of the Reims salient so concerned him that he ordered reserve divisions designated for the long-awaited counteroffensive to reinforce General Berthelot's battered Fifth Army along the Marne. He also ordered preparations for the counteroffensive be suspended until he could better contain the German advance in the west. Pétain realized that Berthelot's army was in no shape to go on the offensive, and until it was brought back up to strength there would be no hope of making the planned counteroffensive the truly decisive double envelopment that Pétain and Foch envisaged.[13]

Foch was irritated when he learned of Pétain's decision to postpone the counteroffensive as he believed that Pétain was being far too cautious and focusing too much on the slight success won by the Germans along the Marne rather than the great French victory won in the east. Foch therefore telephoned Pétain and informed him, "It must be understood that until there are new developments that you will communicate to me, there can be no question at all of slowing up and less so of stopping the [counteroffensive]."[14] Pétain was much chagrined and backed down. Although he disapproved of Foch's decision, he agreed to renew preparations for the counteroffensive with the attack date set for July 18, 1918.

The main blow of Foch's offensive would strike the western flank of the German's Marne salient where the French Sixth Army, under the command of General Degoutte, and the French Tenth Army, under the command of General Mangin, had been concentrating their forces for over a week. Of the two armies, Mangin's held the greater responsibility, for a rapid breakthrough in his sector could capture the critical rail center at Soissons and thus cut off the German Seventh and Ninth armies in their salient before they could disengage from their offensive operations and withdraw.

Pétain insisted that the AEF be given a prominent role in the attack. The French Tenth Army's chief of staff, Gen. Joseph Hellé, recalled, "Pétain wanted [American divisions] associated with the great offensive. He wanted to put them, if only for a few days, in the 'most visible' place of this great offensive action which was the beginning of our victory."[15]

On July 18, 1918, the French Tenth Army and the French Sixth Army attacked the western flank of the German salient along the Marne. The Franco-American XX Corps spearheaded Mangin's Tenth Army assault and was supported by a powerful artillery barrage and approximately 320 French tanks, which provided excellent support to the advancing infantry. The Franco-American forces pushed forward, breaking the thinly held German front line, and advanced as far as eight kilometers in the first day of fighting. The German Ninth Army, charged with defending this sector of the line, was expecting some sort of a localized attack to be launched against it but was unprepared for the massive assault that actually struck its lines. The ferocity of the Americans and their French allies in the attack astounded the Germans, who did not believe that their enemies could recover so quickly from the fighting that had been raging since the opening of the German offensive three days earlier. The Franco-American forces in the Tenth Army captured approximately 7,200 prisoners and twenty one guns in the first day of the attack, and by the end of the day, the flank of the German Ninth Army was in danger of collapsing.[16]

For two days Mangin's Tenth Army and Degoutte's Sixth Army, each with a contingent of two oversized American divisions and supported by armor, drove forward against the western face of the Marne salient. The Germans fought well but were steadily driven back to the vital road and rail line connecting Soissons to Château-Thierry, which the Germans in the Marne salient depended on for their supplies.

Faced with a possible disaster, Crown Prince Wilhelm ordered an abandonment of the Marne bridgeheads and a general withdrawal from the salient. The Germans disengaged from their precarious position astride the Marne before the second wing of the French advance began. The Germans proved themselves, once again, to be tenacious defenders as small groups fought determined rearguard actions that cost the Allies many casualties. Although the Germans were forced to completely abandon their positions along the Marne and lost much heavy equipment and some guns, they managed to extricate the bulk of their forces from the salient before it collapsed. This was in part because General Berthelot's Fifth Army, as Pétain had feared, was not ready when the counteroffensive began and had been forced to wait until July 20, 1918, to go into action.

Although the German armies in the Marne salient were not destroyed, the Second Battle of the Marne was still a great victory for the Allies. The German withdrawal from the Marne marked the end of Germany's bid for victory in the Great War and the beginning of a bloodily futile struggle for survival. Field Marshal Hindenburg later lamented, "How many hopes, cherished during the last few months, had probably collapsed at one blow! How many calculations had been scattered to the winds!"[17] Crown Prince Wilhelm described the Second Battle of the Marne as "the decisive turning point of the war" and later wrote, "I no longer entertained any doubt that matters at the front as well as affairs at home were drifting towards the final catastrophe—a catastrophe which was inevitable."[18]

On August 8, 1918, Field Marshal Haig's BEF launched its own powerful offensive near Amiens, and the German lines cracked wide open. The British began a methodical advance that kept pressure on the retreating Germans and forced them all the way back to the positions they had held in the spring before the great German offensives had begun. As the British attack ran out of steam, Supreme Allied Commander Foch began to commence a buildup for a general offensive to commence in September. He authorized the formation of the U.S. First Army, which, after a brilliant victory at Saint-Mihiel in early September, was placed under Pétain's care as part of a Franco-American army group assigned to the Verdun sector. Pétain assigned more than 100,000 French soldiers to this "American" First Army and provided the nascent American force with a strong complement of tanks and artillery as well. He also demonstrated his faith in Pershing by placing French divisions under American corps and army command.

Foch's general offensive kicked off on September 26, 1918, with British, French, and American armies all going forward simultaneously in the most coordinated Allied effort of the war. The German lines bent and then broke. The BEF made excellent gains in Belgium, where German forces conducted a fighting withdrawal while French and American armies attacked in tandem on either side of the Argonne Forest to make steady advances against fierce German resistance. By the end of October the main German defensive lines had been broken through, and on November 1, 1918, Franco-American forces broke into the open and dashed for the vital rail center of Sedan, threatening to cut off the Germans retreating out of Belgium in the face of the British onslaught.

At this point Pétain readied his Franco-American army group for a new offensive. Using Verdun as their jump-off point, the French and the newly formed U.S. Second Army, which was liberally supplied with French troops and equipment, would attack due east toward the fortress city of Metz, the scene of one of the most horrible defeats in French history in 1870. Metz was the key to reconquering the lost province of Lorraine and driving the Germans from France. Pétain knew its defenses rivaled those of Verdun, and he worried that the coming battle could be a repetition of that grim struggle. With winter on its way, he hoped to take the fortress city in a sudden rush, supported by the fire of large amounts of heavy artillery.

The attack toward Metz began in brisk autumnal weather, and the Franco-American forces made good progress against disorganized German resistance that abruptly stiffened as the Allied forces neared the city. Yet here the battle ended. On November 4, 1918, just as the attack was getting under way, the German High Seas Fleet mutinied rather than conduct a "death ride" sortie into the North Sea. The mutiny sparked a revolution that swept across Germany, and by November 9, as Pétain's guns began to fire on the outlying fortresses of Metz, the kaiser abdicated and Germany's new provisional government requested an armistice. Foch and other French military leaders remained wary, and Pétain was ordered to continue with his attack until a formal document had been signed.

On November 11, 1918, a German delegation arrived at Foch's headquarters to sign the armistice, and messages were at once flashed to all headquarters to cease fire at exactly 11:00 a.m. local time. Pétain was poring over his maps in his headquarters, planning what he knew would be a bloody assault on Metz, when word arrived of the armistice. As Pétain read the message announcing the cease-fire, tears began to well in his eyes. He laid the missive aside, buried his face in his hands, and began weeping uncontrollably. The Great War was over at long last.

5

Between World Wars, 1918–1939

The commanding generals of the victorious Allied armies gathered at the ancient fortress city of Metz on December 8, 1918, to honor one of their own. The city had been taken by the Germans as part of the spoils of their victory in the Franco-Prussian War in 1871, and the German Empire had ruled it for more than four decades. Now Metz, along with the rest of the lost areas of Lorraine, celebrated the return of the French army in November 1918. Pétain, mounted on a white horse, led a triumphal procession of French soldiers into town to the wild adulation of the liberated populace. On the Esplanade de Metz, beneath the statue honoring Napoleon's "bravest of the brave," Marshal Michel Ney, Pétain received his marshal's baton from President Raymond Poincaré and Premier Georges Clemenceau.

The ceremony was one of many marking the Allied victory in the Great War that Pétain had participated in, as over the next few months he was caught up in a whirlwind of parades and celebrations. On July 14, 1919, France celebrated Bastille Day with a momentous ceremony to mark the hard-won victory in the Great War. Contingents from all of the Allied armies, led by their commanding generals, marched down the Champs-Élysées. The crowd in Paris cheered them all but reserved their greatest outburst of emotion and applause for their own soldiers. Pétain, mounted on a white horse and carrying his marshal's baton in his right hand, led the French soldiers whose units represented every department in France. It was the crowning moment of the marshal's long and illustrious career of service to France, and he was at that point ready to quietly ease into retirement with the crowd's cheers still reverberating in his ears.

Pétain had always dreamed of retiring to his native Pas-de-Calais and settling down to the life of a gentleman farmer. But when the time had come at last, industrialization and the radical leftist politics of the labor unions that had set up shop there had changed the region so much that it was no longer attractive to him. He purchased a home and some land in the Midi instead, where he set up a modest farm, which he dubbed *l'Ermitage*. He was not good at farming and quipped that it would have been cheaper for him to go to the market and purchase his food rather than trying to grow it himself.

In 1920 the lifelong bachelor married Eugénie Hardon, even though up to the last minute he had maintained serious relationships with several other ladies. In some circles, for example, with his good friend and best man Émile Fayolle, his civil marriage ceremony to a divorcée raised a few eyebrows. However, to many, his eschewing of Roman Catholic principles reaffirmed Pétain's republican credentials and consequently raised his status even further in the public eye. At a personal level, the marriage slowed Pétain's philandering ways but never halted them. Though he was now in his mid-sixties, he maintained relationships with a number of far younger mistresses throughout the 1920s and 1930s.

Pétain's retirement proved to be short lived. In 1920 the government appointed him vice president of the Conseil Supérieur de la Guerre, a position that in time of war converted to the post of commander in chief of the French army. Thus, he found himself once more active in the public sphere. In his new post, Pétain dedicated himself to fighting against the rapid demobilization of the French army. His task was a losing proposition from the first. France was a democracy and the people demanded their soldiers be returned home. With the horrific struggle just over, no one wanted to hear about preparing for future conflicts. Pétain knew, however, that the only way France could avoid another war was to maintain its standing, acquired as a result of its victory in the war, as the foremost military power in Europe. That military power was based on the French army, but it was evaporating before Pétain's eyes as the French Left in particular called for a drastic reduction in the army's size and in the length of service for conscripts from three years to eighteen months.

Even as the army was being demobilized, a succession of French governments insisted on increasing the nation's military commitments by establishing the so-called *petite Entente* of alliances with new nations created at Versailles, such as Czechoslovakia and Poland. These countries were formed around Germany to keep the country diplomatically isolated and to serve as a buffer against future German aggression. Pétain viewed these new Allied countries as dangerous. He believed they offered France little but asked much in the way of defense commitments of its dwindling armed forces. Petite Entente worked for the time being, while Germany lay prostrate and disarmed. Yet Pétain knew Germany would want to regain its strength, and the only way to enforce the Treaty of Versailles was with a powerful military force capable of offensive action. The government would not grant him this, and Pétain became increasingly pessimistic about what the future held for France.

When war came again to Pétain it broke out in an unexpected place, Morocco. Morocco was a region with soaring mountains, blazing deserts, and quarreling tribes. The French and Spanish had conquered it in the early 1900s and established their own colonial zones of influence, though officially Morocco was a protectorate of France. In 1919 a rebellion broke out in a region known as the Rif, which lay in the Spanish zone. At first it seemed like a routine colonial uprising, but the Spanish army and government reacted sluggishly to the threat, and after a string of small successes against their Spanish overlords, the rebels and their charismatic leader Abd el-Krim won over many tribes to their cause. The rebellion turned into a full-scale conflict, which became known as the Rif War. The French initially allowed the Spanish to handle the problem, which was isolated to the Spanish zones, while they worked to make sure their own zones were secure and the tribes friendly to France remained loyal. But in 1924 the Riffian forces scored a series of stunning victories over the Spanish army.

The Spanish suffered heavy casualties in these battles and also lost hundreds of artillery pieces and machine guns, which Krim immediately used to arm his own forces. The victory caused much of the Moroccan population to throw its allegiance behind the rebels, and Krim's ranks were further bolstered by deserters from the Spanish and French garrisons, as well as European mercenaries who brought much-needed technical skills to his armed forces. Instead of a lightly armed "native" force, Krim now possessed an army and consequently raised the stakes. His dream was to liberate all of Morocco from European rule, and to do that he needed to strike at the French.

In 1925 Riffian forces staged a number of attacks against the French outposts that guarded the western frontier of their North African possessions. French bases were overrun and their garrisons were gruesomely slaughtered. The colonial governor was Marshal Louis-Hubert-Gonzalve Lyautey, a brilliantly eccentric personality who personified the French Empire in North Africa and was widely regarded as France's greatest colonial soldier. Yet even he had never dealt with a threat so serious before. He cabled Paris to say that his forces were inadequate to hold Morocco and also cautioned that there was a danger that Krim's successes could spark further Berber and Arab revolts throughout French North Africa. Premier Paul Painlevé received this news with considerable alarm and immediately summoned Marshal Pétain.

Painlevé shared the intelligence he had on the uprising with Pétain and then asked him to go to Morocco and take command of French forces there. Pétain protested that he was not a colonial soldier and had no experience in such matters. He also said that at age sixty-nine he was getting too old to take an active field command. Painlevé waved off these protestations and told Pétain that he was the only man in France who could salvage the situation. At length Pétain agreed to go, but with grave reservations. In his advanced years, Pétain was acutely aware of his place in French history and wished to maintain it. He had already won a formidable reputation and crushing a colonial revolt could do little to add to it. However, if he failed to overcome the natives, a black mark would forever stain his record. Still, France had called, and once more Pétain answered.

Pétain determined that the campaign could be effective only if there were direct military cooperation between French and Spanish forces. He therefore first went to Madrid, where he met with Gen. Miguel Primo de Rivera, the military dictator of Spain. The two men hit it off quite well and reached an agreement on Pétain's plan for a large joint military operation against the rebels that would take place in the spring of the following year. Pétain's next stop was in Fez, Morocco, where he met with Marshal Lyautey. The colonial soldier had expected reinforcements, but not a marshal to come with them. Realizing that he was essentially being replaced as commander, Lyautey tendered his resignation and announced he would return to France. Pétain assured him that this was a temporary state of affairs, and France still had great need of his administrative abilities in the colonies once the war was over. Lyautey appreciated this and then asked if he could remain in Fez as an adviser, a suggestion to which Pétain readily assented.

At Pétain's request, French reinforcements poured into North Africa. By spring they totaled more than 150,000 troops liberally equipped with machine guns and heavy artillery and detachments of light tanks and bombers. Pétain took the initial complement of these forces and threw them into a spoiling attack against the Rif that fall. The objective was to cauterize Algeria's western frontier and force the Riffians to the defensive. Pétain's forces moved slowly and methodically. He isolated Rif strongholds and villages and then pounded them into submission with artillery and aerial bombardment. These operations continued until the winter rains brought active campaigning to a halt. By that time, the major rebel bases had been either destroyed or isolated, and Franco-Spanish forces were poised to administer the coup de grâce with the joint offensive Pétain had planned earlier that year. Pétain announced his work in North Africa was done, and he returned to Paris, where he gave a rousing speech proclaiming victory in the Rif War. His detractors pointed out that Abd el-Krim was still at large and his army was still numerous and dangerous. Pétain shrugged off these objections for he knew the writing was on the wall, and indeed it was.

On April 15, 1926, French and Spanish forces launched the offensive designed by Pétain the previous year. They combined an amphibious landing by Spanish troops in the north with a powerful drive in the south by Pétain's newly created mechanized juggernaut. After putting up a spirited defense, the Riffians abruptly collapsed in the face of this onslaught and retreated back into their mountain strongholds. Even there they found no peace; they were pursued by Franco-Spanish forces, and under constant aerial attack, Krim at length surrendered to the French on May 27, 1926. The war came to an end.

It is important to note that in light of later criticism of Pétain as being a moribund strategic thinker wedded to a defense at all costs doctrine, the Rif War demonstrated his true abilities. Although completely unfamiliar with North Africa, he nevertheless organized a coalition of Franco-Spanish forces to deal with the rebellion and used armor and air in a combined operations offensive, which he tied in with an amphibious attack. The campaign vividly demonstrated that his abilities as an army commander were yet undiminished by age and that unlike other commanders of his generation, his ideas were forward thinking and innovative in terms of using the new technology available on the battlefield.

The Rif War was a thunderous success, but Pétain was disturbed by what he saw when he returned to Paris. Much to his disgust he learned that, rather than celebrating the French victory, leftist members of the Chamber of Deputies had condemned the war and the French army's participation in it. Whatever his thoughts about politics, Pétain was certain of one thing: in time of war national unity was imperative for victory and survival. He had disapproved, but tolerated, the Left's excesses in the first part of the decade, but this latest outrage appears to have deeply affected him. He became extremely concerned about the Left's negative influence in French culture and its increasing embrace of communism, socialism, and pacifism, even to the point of denigrating the French victory in the Great War as being nothing but a massacre of the workers and peasants for no good reason. These themes had become especially apparent in the nation's schools, and Pétain worried about the impact such teachings were having on the next generation of soldiers who would have to defend the Republic. In private he increasingly denounced the "communist schoolteachers" of France, who, he believed, were eating away at the moral and spiritual fortitude of France with their leftist teachings.

By way of contrast with these developments in his own country, Pétain had been greatly impressed by Primo de Rivera. Spain had long ceased to be one of the great powers of Europe, but under Primo de Rivera's leadership the nation appeared to be revitalized and have a new sense of purpose. The Spanish army's ultimate triumph, with French assistance, of course, in the Rif War was evidence that it had greatly increased in quality and that the nation it represented was on the rise. As Pétain became increasingly concerned about the Left's malignant influence in France, he became fascinated with the new authoritarian regimes taking hold in Europe. It would be too much to say that Pétain became a fascist, for he never thought deeply enough about political matters to warrant a codification of his beliefs. Yet there is no question that he became infatuated with how a strong authoritarian leader, appealing to his people to return to the foundation of their national greatness and to reject the socialists and communists, could reinvigorate the French and motivate them to greatness. He saw it firsthand in Spain and also saw a similar occurrence with the rise to power of Benito Mussolini's regime in Italy. Meanwhile, his own nation, with more military power and political influence and with much more to offer the world than either Italy or Spain as far as he was concerned, was teetering on a precipice of complete collapse thanks to Marxism's influence. All of this weighed heavily on his mind for many years to come.

In 1925 Pétain renewed his relationship with Charles de Gaulle. De Gaulle, now a major, was assigned to Pétain's personal staff, much to the initial delight of both him and Pétain. De Gaulle still greatly admired Pétain and in fact had named his first-born son "Philippe" in the marshal's honor. However, de Gaulle had matured considerably in the decade that had passed since he was a second lieutenant in Pétain's regiment. He had served in combat and been wounded at Verdun, where he was captured and had spent two years as a prisoner of war in Germany. His most recent assignment was as an instructor of military history at the Saint-Cyr Military Academy. He had devoted much study and thought to the art of war since then as well and, having found that he had a gift for writing, had begun to put his ideas down in a series of articles.

As an author, de Gaulle found himself assigned to Pétain's team of "ghostwriters." Pétain was not much of an author himself, so he employed younger officers to put his thoughts down in various articles and even had them write the prefaces for books that he had been requested to provide introductions for. Pétain served mainly as an editor for these pieces, and he went over the articles meticulously, providing editorial suggestions and comments that were then incorporated into the piece before it was published. Although he denied his ghostwriters a byline, Pétain always gave them half the revenue he received for his writings.

Pétain assigned de Gaulle to write a book on the history of the French army. Unbeknownst to Pétain, de Gaulle had already begun such a work before he was assigned to the marshal's staff. De Gaulle completed the work in short order and dutifully submitted the chapters to Pétain for his editorial comments. Much to Pétain's chagrin, however, de Gaulle refused to implement all of the marshal's editorial instructions and argued with him over the work's scope and tone. After a while de Gaulle tired of the argument and announced to Pétain that the book was completed. Pétain disagreed; it would be finished when he said it was. The two argued at length over the subject, and what had begun as a seemingly trivial affair degenerated into a serious dispute between the two men.

Eventually, de Gaulle requested to be reassigned from Pétain's staff, a request that was readily granted. But it did not end there, for de Gaulle contracted with a publisher to have the manuscript published. Pétain immediately protested that the work, which he had collaborated on, was not written for general distribution, and he demanded that he be listed as a coauthor of the book. After much dispute, de Gaulle agreed to allow Pétain to write a formal introduction and dedication for the work, and Pétain grumblingly assented to this compromise. Yet he delayed in sending it in, and by the time it arrived, the book had already gone to press with a dedication written by de Gaulle instead. It was generously worded, but it was not the piece Pétain had written himself and did not give the marshal full credit as coauthor of the entire work. When Pétain saw that it had been published without his own personal introduction, he was furious and the rift between the two men never healed.

In 1927 Pétain was asked to deliver the dedication speech at the formal opening of the *ossuaire* at the Verdun battlefield. Just eleven years after the titanic struggle, the battlefield was still a shell-pocked wasteland, but this did not deter a massive throng numbered in the hundreds of thousands to turn out for a series of commemorative activities that marked the monument's opening. The ceremonies culminated with a long funeral procession that bore the unidentified remains of French and German soldiers from their temporary graves throughout Verdun up the winding road to their final resting place in the ossuaire. The day was appropriately dark and rainy, and the emphasis was on the sacrifice the French soldiers had made during the battle that had led to the victory there. Of all the numerous speakers, the "Victor of Verdun" was the one most eagerly anticipated by the crowd.

Pétain's remarks eschewed references to himself or the senior leadership of the French army and instead focused on "the soldier of Verdun." He reminded the crowd that the soldier of 1916 was not a starry-eyed inexperienced idealist. Rather the soldier of Verdun was a veteran whose "long practice in fighting had taught him that success is to the most tenacious, and had developed in him qualities of patience and persistence." He told his listeners that the French soldier fought out of a sense of duty and felt that he "carried the burden of his country's need, more important than his own, [and] he did his duty to the very limit of his powers." He also reminded his listeners that the people needed to support their fighting men and added, "It is impossible to believe that the soldier could have risen to such heights of heroism if he had not felt behind him the inspiration of the whole nation. . . . It was only because the soldier had the spirit of the nation behind him to drive him on that he won the battle. It was his country's will that he fulfilled."[1]

Verdun was never far from Pétain's mind. In his final years as commanding general he threw his full support behind a plan for national defense based on his experiences in the battle. Pétain and others proposed the construction of a massive belt of fortifications, resembling those at Verdun, to defend the newly liberated provinces of Alsace and eastern Lorraine and protect the nation's frontier with Germany. Sited on advantageous terrain and incorporating all of the hard-earned lessons of the Battle of Verdun, the fortresses would be the most formidable defensive works ever built.

The proposal called for modern forts built of reinforced concrete, with multiple machine-gun and artillery pieces in hardened disappearing turrets that would be impervious to even the heaviest bombardment. Vast labyrinths of underground galleries would be constructed beneath the surface to house the garrison, and the air inside the forts would be pressurized to prevent poison gas from penetrating it. Huge storage galleries would contain enough food, water, and ammunition to hold out indefinitely. These fortifications would become known to history as the "Maginot Line."

Although heavily criticized through the lens of history, at the time the arguments in favor of building the Maginot Line were sound. All French military planners agreed that the next war would involve a German invasion of France that would have to be defeated in a defensive battle. As they fought the invader to a standstill, France would mobilize the resources of its overseas empire as well as muster foreign support from Britain and possibly the United States. Once this mobilization had been achieved, a counteroffensive would be launched that would bring the final victory. To provide the time needed for mobilization the French would have to fight and win the initial defensive battle. As they searched for a model of what they wanted to accomplish they could find no better example of a defensive victory than the greatest French battle of World War I, Verdun.

During the Battle of Verdun the forts had formed the centers of resistance and had proved critical to the French victory. Pétain argued that a lack of faith in the forts' defensive advantages had nearly led to disaster at Verdun. Although disparaged by the French high command, the French troops themselves had discovered that the concrete walls of their forts, however inadequate and outmoded, provided far superior protection and observation posts than anything offered by improvised field fortifications. He also pointed out that only two forts had fallen to the Germans during the battle: Fort Douaumont had been lost because the French had failed to man it properly, and Fort Vaux was lost when the garrison ran out of water. Pétain stated that under the new plans, neither of the failures would ever occur.

French poster from 1917, "The Military Power of France"

Pétain in 1918

Pétain with American general John J. Pershing in 1918

Pétain in 1917

Gen. Joseph Joffre and President Raymond Poincaré visit Pétain's headquarters at Souilly during the Battle of Verdun

Pétain decorates a U.S. soldier in 1918 as General Pershing looks on

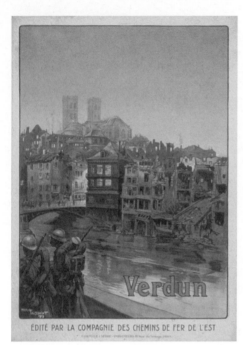

Verdun poster

Unidentified human remains prior to their interment in the Ossuaire at Verdun

Fortified entrance to Tour et Pont Chausée at Verdun

German gunners at Verdun eating lunch

On ne passé pas poster

*Fort Vaux after
its recapture in
November 1916*

German prisoners captured at Verdun

Midnight mass inside Fort Douaumont, 1916

Paul Painlevé, the French minister of war who made Petain commander in chief of the French army in 1917

Maginot Line gun turrets, 1936

Pétain in 1940

Other considerations favored the building of the defensive line and perhaps foremost among these was demographics. The French nation had lost 1.4 million men in battle during the Great War, and another million young men returned as permanently disabled veterans. French population growth had been at near zero prior to this catastrophe, and in the interwar period it dropped to dangerously low levels. Any army the French high command fielded in a future war would be decidedly smaller than the one it had in 1914–1918. Pétain and his supporters argued that the only way to compensate for this was to use fortifications to magnify the fighting power of the troops France would have. This did not mean that Pétain saw no value in other arms, including tanks and aircraft. To the contrary, Pétain wrote, "A fortification alone is not enough to check the enemy, but it greatly increases the resisting strength of troops who know how to use it."[2] To his way of thinking, the fortresses were always part of the plan for halting the next invasion and protecting France's vital areas from the enemy, but he never envisioned them to be the sole basis for national defense.

The other argument that supported the building of the Maginot Line was political in nature. The Left in France grew in strength and number throughout the 1920s and 1930s, and its staunch opposition to military spending and war planning grew in proportion to its power. Tanks and aircraft were offensive weapons and therefore could be used for wars of aggression or foreign adventures that the Left was determined to keep France out of. In contrast, fortifications were by definition purely defensive and could not be used for such endeavors. Consequently, when defense spending was discussed in the Chamber of Deputies, funds for aircraft and armor were slashed, while even the most die-hard leftist had trouble summoning up arguments against a system of fortifications to defend the republic. Ideally, Pétain would have liked to have had both the forts and the offensive weapons, but he realized that in peacetime that was not possible. Since he had to choose, he believed the forts should come first while the armored units and aircraft formations could be mobilized once the war started.

In 1930 Minister of War André Maginot secured the final political support for the construction of the series of forts that would bear his name. When it was completed in 1935 the Maginot Line ran from

Switzerland to Luxembourg and covered the entire frontier with Germany. The defense system ended at the Ardennes Forest, leaving northern France open and unprotected. Unlike Alsace and Lorraine, northern France was heavily industrialized and contained several large metropolitan centers. The construction of defensive barriers and fortresses in this region would have severely disrupted the local economy and civilian population. Also, France had a military alliance with Belgium, and the French had given solemn assurances to the Belgians that they would intervene if the Germans attacked. If the Maginot Line extended the length of the Belgian border, it would give the impression that the French were content to stay put in their fortresses and concede Belgium to the Germans. The final consideration in terms of the wall's length was cost, and in the long run this became the final arbiter. The Maginot Line was already the costliest defense project ever undertaken by the Third Republic, and it was estimated that it would cost almost three times what had already been spent to extend the line all the way to the English Channel. As the Great Depression began to eat away at the French economy in the 1930s, funds for such exorbitantly expensive projects were in short supply.

Pétain took all of these factors into consideration, and shortly before retiring he developed a plan for war that made the best use of the Maginot Line as well as the mobile forces France possessed. His final scheme envisaged that the bulk of the French army would mass along the Belgian frontier with its right flank secured by the Maginot Line and the natural barrier of the Ardennes Forest. As a crisis with Germany loomed, his armies would move into Belgium, under the terms of their alliance, and advance to the Dyle River. Once there they would establish defensive positions in concert with their Belgian allies to stop the inevitable German replay of the Great War's Schlieffen Plan. This strategy would ensure that Belgium, and not northern France, would be the theater of war. The region would also serve as the staging area for the envisioned counteroffensive, which, with British and hopefully American support, would defeat the Germans. Thus, the Maginot Line would be the shield of France, manned by conscripts and ensuring the safety and territorial integrity of the eastern frontier. Meanwhile, the professional element of the French army, which included its best divisions and most of its armor, would be the sword that would parry the enemy thrust and then drive into the Rhineland and defeat Germany.[3]

As construction of the Maginot Line got under way, Pétain made frequent inspection tours of the construction sites and offered his advice and insights whenever possible. He had decided to retire and saw the fortresses as his final legacy to the nation; they would provide for its defense after he was gone. His retirement came in 1930, when, at age seventy-four, he at last relinquished his post as commander in chief of the French army. He had spent more than half a century in service to France and had seen it through the greatest trial in its long and troubled history. It was now time to at last step off the stage of history and allow younger men to carry on the work of defending *la grand nation*.

Pétain quickly grew to enjoy his retirement. In 1931 he was formally inducted into the prestigious Académie française, whose ultra-elite membership was limited to forty people who represented the best of France in the government, business, the arts, and, of course, the military. Later that same year he was asked to head the French mission sent to the United States for the festivities held in honor of the 150th anniversary of the Franco-American victory at Yorktown, the battle that had won America's independence from Great Britain.

As the Great Depression spread across the Western world, France, which had been initially spared from its consequences, began to feel the pinch. Defense spending was among the first casualties of fiscal belt tightening, and as a cost-saving measure the annual military maneuvers were cancelled in 1932 and again in 1933. The government dramatically cut wages for both officers and soldiers, and the French army began to shrink in size. The world's most formidable military force throughout the 1920s was now beginning to fall into disrepair. The only bright note was that work still continued apace on the Maginot Line, and this was no small consolation to the French high command as it prepared to enter the so-called hollow years of the French army.

The term was in reference to the fact that the French birthrate, sluggish for a century, had been cut in half during the years 1915 to 1919 and had made only slight gains since, still not approaching its pre-1914 levels. Thus, beginning with the class of 1935, the French army could expect only 120,000 new recruits instead of the 240,000 it was accustomed to, and this trend would continue for another five years at least. As a result, the French army would not only be hard pressed to maintain its position as the foremost army in the world, it would be extremely difficult to field even the minimal force deemed necessary for national defense.

Economic problems in France soon led to political turmoil, and after a series of financial scandals rocked the government of Premier Edouard Daladier, a massive demonstration was held in protest of the government's poor handling of the affairs on February 6, 1934. The demonstrators belonged to various right-wing groups including the World War I veteran's organization the Croix de Feu and the Action Française, which was staunchly Catholic and favored a restoration of the Orléanist constitutional monarchy. They received support from the old royalist Marshal Lyautey, who in his waning days thought he had found his cause at last.

During the course of the demonstrations, the police at the scene panicked and opened fire on the crowd, killing dozens and wounding more than three hundred. It was a shocking development and resulted in an outcry from all corners of the French political spectrum against the government. At the height of the crisis, Lyautey visited Pétain and told him the conflict could end in a revolution and the overthrow of the government. If that became the case, Lyautey said, he wanted to be able to count on Pétain's support. Pétain refused Lyautey and said that he would not participate in any insurrection against the republic. Whether he did so, as his supporters later claimed, out of loyalty to France or, as his detractors claimed, because it would have placed Lyautey in charge instead of himself, will never be known. Regardless, the two parted on cordial terms and appeared to have reached an understanding on the matter.

The Third Republic survived the demonstrations, but Daladier's government did not. He was forced to resign, and a coalition government under Gaston Doumergue took his place. Doumergue tried to form a stable government with leaders from both the Left and the Right. He knew that the Right trusted no one more than Pétain and that of all the military figures in France the Left found Pétain to be the least objectionable. Doumergue asked Pétain, who was seventy-eight, to join his new government as the minister of war, and after a lengthy debate the marshal reluctantly agreed to leave retirement behind and accepted the post.

On assuming his duties as minister of war, Pétain threw his full prestige behind obtaining more funds for the army, a task in which he was partially successful. Having obtained additional funds, one of his first steps was to order the resumption of the annual summer maneuvers, which he deemed to be critically important. He also attempted to address the manpower issues brought about by the "hollow years" by requesting that military service for all conscripts be extended from one year to three. He also requested additional funding to recruit volunteers for the army and to retain noncommissioned officers and junior officers, who were leaving the army because of poor morale and substandard pay.

His arguments for improving and expanding the French army took on a new meaning in 1935, when Adolf Hitler renounced the Versailles treaty and began to rearm Germany. Pétain's speeches took on a strident tone as he tried to explain that the French military force of the 1920s was designed to contain a disarmed and docile Germany. Important measures had to be taken immediately if France was to meet this new threat from its old foe.

Pétain ran into serious opposition from the Left, which was determined to prevent an arms race with the Germans. The Left also opposed the emergence of a powerful professional army, which it believed would inevitably ally itself with the reactionary elements of the Right to threaten the republic's integrity. Pétain was angered and frustrated by this opposition from within, especially because the threat from across the frontier, long feared, was now emerging with a vengeance. The clamor of discordant voices from across the political spectrum troubled him. Politicians of every stripe appeared more intent on defeating their political opponents rather than looking to the good of the nation. This was Pétain's first real experience with political infighting, and he was disgusted by it.

He also grew more alarmed by the Left's influence on the young people of France. French schoolteachers and academics had become overwhelmingly leftist in outlook, and their teaching of pacifist and socialist principles instead of the traditional virtues of patriotism and national service was, in Pétain's view, undermining France's moral foundation. At one point while serving as the minister of war, in 1935, Pétain exclaimed, "I'll be happy to take on the Education Ministry as well as War. I'll handle those Communist schoolteachers!"[4]

Tired of the political bickering, Pétain tendered his resignation as minister of war in 1935. Yet Doumergue felt his administration could not lose the marshal's prestige and so begged him to accept the post of minister of air defense. Doumergue told Pétain he could focus on exclusively military matters and not be burdened with the political infighting that had proven to be so unpleasant to him. Pétain accepted the post and with characteristic enthusiasm hurled himself into his new duties. Although he was seventy-nine years old and had spent his entire military career as an infantryman, he had developed a strong appreciation for the importance of airpower, especially during his defense of Verdun. At a time when other French military theorists, including de Gaulle, were arguing the merits of armored warfare to the exclusion of other developments, Pétain stated that without airpower the tanks would be useless. With enough quality aircraft, Pétain argued, he could nail an opponent's mechanized forces to the ground and destroy them from above. This was a prophetic statement: a central ingredient of the German blitzkrieg of 1939–1941 was aerial supremacy. The loss of that aerial supremacy on the battlefield in 1944 resulted in the German armored formations, in spite of their superior tanks, being helpless before the aerial onslaught of the Allies.

Pétain was weary of voicing arguments that no one wanted to hear, and as he grew older he lacked the patience and the will to continue these political battles. As German soldiers marched into the Rhineland, in direct violation of the Treaty of Versailles, the Left took control of the French government with the Popular Front in 1936. Pétain decided his career was over and hoped that the measures he had taken for the defense of his nation, especially the Maginot Line and improvements in aircraft design, would suffice.

He remained in retirement until the auspicious year of 1939, when a new French government under the returned Daladier asked him to become ambassador to Spain. The Fascists under Gen. Francisco Franco had won the Spanish Civil War, and Daladier, concerned about Franco's relationship with Germany and Italy, sought to protect France's southern flank through cordial relations with the new government. Pétain had worked with the Spanish successfully during the Rif War, and it was hoped he could draw on that relationship to keep Spain neutral in the conflict that was rapidly approaching in Europe.

Pétain accepted the appointment and presented his credentials to Franco. The two had met during the Rif War when Franco was a junior officer, and they established a strong relationship. Pétain could not help but express his admiration, and envy, of the peace and stability that Franco's rule had given to Spain. Pétain looked favorably on its restoration of traditional Spanish values of the soil, the church, and national service and on its destruction and repudiation of the communists, who had threatened all of these things. In Spain he saw this accomplished by a strong military leader, much like his friend Primo de Rivera, and he often voiced his regret that France did not have a similar political system. The coalition that ruled France now, with Daladier at its head, was repugnant to him. Pétain believed that as the pathetically weak and divided Third Republic muddled its way through a series of diplomatic crises with Hitler's resurgent Germany, it was headed toward destruction, and he could only hope it did not take France down with it.

6

The Fall of France, Vichy, and Exile

On September 1, 1939, Germany invaded Poland. France and Great Britain, at last determined to make a stand against Hitler's aggression, declared war on Germany two days later. Pétain was in Madrid when he received news of the outbreak of hostilities and immediately voiced his displeasure to those around him. He exclaimed that France was unprepared for war as the army had too few tanks and aircraft, and he believed Premier Daladier's government was ill-suited to lead France in wartime. Though Daladier heard about these comments, he nevertheless asked Pétain to come to Paris and resume his old post as minister of war in the new cabinet he was forming.

Pétain arrived in Paris and soon made it clear to anyone who would listen that he believed the war was a mistake. He also did not care for the leftist politicians Daladier was including in the new government and expressed his concerns that these individuals would cause trouble for France with the fascist regimes of neutral Italy and Spain. Pétain also expressed his reservations about Gen. Maurice Gamelin's abilities to command the French army. If anyone was expecting the "Victor of Verdun" to spring forth sword in hand to defend the republic, he was sorely disappointed. That Pétain was gone, and in his place was an old, tired man whose heart was not in this fight. Pétain concluded his meetings with a disappointed Daladier by refusing the post of minister of war. He told the premier he felt that as an outsider he would be able to give better advice to than if he were a member of the government, and with that he returned his ambassadorial duties in Spain.

The French and British spent the winter of 1939–1940 waiting and scheming while they yielded the initiative of events to Hitler. Public resentment in France against Daladier's inept handling of the war reached a crescendo until, assailed by opponents from the Left and the Right, Daladier's government collapsed and was replaced by that of Paul Reynaud. As Daladier had, Reynaud attempted to rally the nation around its glorious military past by requesting that Marshal Pétain, France's greatest living hero, join his government as minister of state. Once more, however, Pétain decided to maintain his distance, at least for the time being, while he waited to see how events played out with Reynaud's new government and the war.

On May 10, 1940, Germany struck in the West, invading Holland and Belgium in what appeared to many as a repeat of the Schlieffen Plan of World War I. General Gamelin ordered a general advance into Belgium with approximately 60 percent of the French army and the BEF to stop the German onslaught. The Allies concentrated on the perceived threat advancing through Holland and northern Belgium, but failed to notice the buildup of German armor near the Ardennes Forest in southeast Belgium.

On May 14, 1940, Gen. Heinz Guderian's 48th Panzer Corps launched a powerful armored assault through the Ardennes Forest and headed for Sedan, where the French mobile forces joined with their Maginot Line garrisons. With their eyes fixated on the north, the French never saw the attack coming, and Guderian's panzers smashed through the thinly held French defenses. German infantry and artillery followed the panzers and consolidated their bridgehead along the Meuse as they prepared to make their next move. On May 16 Guderian's forces broke out of the Meuse bridgehead and attacked northwest. Guderian's swift-moving panzers struck across the rear of the Anglo-French forces in Belgium, overrunning supply depots, disrupting communications, and threatening to cut off the main Allied armies. The French army's maneuvers remained ponderously slow and hopelessly unimaginative during this critical moment. The French high command was stunned by the speed and decisiveness of the German breakthrough at Sedan and was unable to quickly adapt and develop a proper plan of action to deal with this unforeseen event. The vast bulk of Gamelin's armored forces were soon cut off in Belgium, and he had retained no mobile reserve that could have been used for a counteroffensive. In addition Gamelin, under political pressure to be sure, insisted that a strong screening force remain in place before Paris, even though the German panzers were clearly heading for the English Channel and away from the French capital. Gamelin also refused to withdraw any forces from the Maginot Line; they remained pinned in their fortifications by orders and prewar doctrine rather than German pressure. Indeed, it was the slow movement of French forces, matched by Gamelin's and slow decision-making process that sealed the fate of the Allied forces in Belgium.

As the French high command watched in bewildered amazement, the Germans swiftly advanced to the northwest and completely cut off the main French army, along with the entire BEF. If the French high command failed to act, the French government was determined to do something, anything, to retrieve the situation. Intent on rallying the army and nation, Premier Reynaud shuffled his government and the army's high command. He sacked Gamelin and replaced him with Gen. Maxime Weygand, the former chief of staff of the late Marshal Foch, and then sent a summons to Marshal Pétain in Madrid asking him to return to France at once for an important assignment.

Pétain received Reynaud's summons calmly. He knew from earlier reports that the situation in France was serious, but the message made it clear that the republic was staring disaster square in the face. If that was indeed the case, then Pétain believed he had no choice but to serve his country. He went to see the Spanish dictator, General Franco, to announce his resignation as ambassador. Pétain told Franco, "My country has been beaten and they are calling me back to make peace and to sign an armistice. . . . This is the work of thirty years of Marxism."[1]

Pétain arrived in Paris on May 18, 1940. Reynaud offered him the position of vice premier, and he accepted. That night Reynaud went on the radio to address a desperate nation and informed the people that the

German breakthrough along the Meuse had become more serious and that the republic was in dire peril. However, all was not lost, and in fact he had already taken firm steps to rectify the situation. To that end, Reynaud announced, "The Victor of Verdun, Marshal Pétain, returned this morning from Madrid. He will now be at my side . . . putting all his wisdom and all his force in the service of his country. He will remain there until victory is won."[2]

The French press hailed Reynaud's announcement of Pétain's presence in the government. From the standpoint of building national morale in a time of crisis, the arrival of Pétain in Paris and the assumption of command by Weygand, two individuals intimately associated with France's victory in the Great War, were joyful news to a nation desperate for salvation. Yet many in the French army and government saw the situation more clearly. Weygand was seventy-four, and while he was a superb staff officer during the Great War, he had no real experience with independent command. Pétain was eighty-four, and while Reynaud intended for him to be the chief consultant on military affairs, the marshal had no knowledge of the rapidly developing campaign in France at the time of his appointment.

Pétain's role was extremely limited in his new position, and he had no direct control or influence over military or political matters. It quickly became clear to him that he was being used mainly as a symbol, a rallying point for a French nation teetering on the precipice of defeat, yet with no authority to influence the outcome of events. Some who saw him during those days commented on his lethargy and even speculated as to whether senility had crept in. In fact, at this time he appears to have fallen into a pattern of slipping in and out of coherency. He could be quite lucid, yet at other times he was seemingly completely out of touch with reality. While at eighty-four he was certainly not at the peak of his powers, it should also be noted that his actual duties were vague and offered no avenue for action even if he had possessed his full faculties.

In northern France a stunned French army seemed powerless to shake out of the lethargy imposed on it by its own leaders and the stunning swiftness with which the Germans were exploiting their breakthrough along the Meuse. The Germans tightened the noose around the Allied forces in Belgium, and on May 29, King Leopold III of Belgium announced the surrender of his nation. The following day the British began to evacuate the BEF and French soldiers from the pocket through the French port of Dunkirk. There was some hope that these evacuated forces could be transported to southern France and re-formed, but the British decided instead to transport everyone to Britain. This was a sound decision for while enough transport was found to get most of the soldiers out, the British and French were forced to abandon their heavy equipment, tanks, and artillery on the beaches. Thus, it was not an army that arrived in Britain, but a demoralized, and almost totally unequipped, mass of humanity. The soldiers had escaped the German trap but for all intents and purposes were out of the campaign for the foreseeable future.

As the evacuation from Dunkirk began, the French high command and government waited tensely for the next phase of the German operation that would inevitably be aimed south toward Paris. Less than half the French army remained to face this onslaught as their best divisions and most of their armor had been trapped in Belgium. General Weygand took what was left and deployed them along the so-called Weygand Line, a porous and totally unprepared defensive position that ran along the Somme and Aisne rivers and was anchored on the westernmost fortifications of the Maginot Line.

An increasingly distraught Pétain visited Paul Baudouin, Reynaud's deputy secretary of state and secretary of the War Cabinet, on May 26. Pétain was in a foul mood when he arrived and voiced his displeasure over Reynaud's announcement that fifteen generals had been relieved of command. The marshal blamed the defeat on former premier Daladier's failed policies, and he refused to hold the French army responsible. As Pétain contemplated the course the war would now take, he told Baudoin, "It is easy, but also stupid, to talk of fighting to the last man: it is also criminal, in view of our losses in the last war and of our low birth-rate." He emphasized the necessity of saving at least part of the army, for without it there would be nothing around which the defeated nation could begin to rebuild. Pétain's eyes brimmed with tears as he said that he was eighty-four years old and had spent his whole life in service to France. It was a cruel fate, he told Baudouin, that in his final years he had to serve her under such "awful circumstances."[3]

In the midst of this crisis, rumors were rife that, with the BEF evacuated, Reynaud's government might break the alliance with Britain and sign a separate peace with the Germans. Pétain had maintained his intense distrust and dislike for the British since World War I. On June 4 Pétain told the American ambassador to France, William Bullitt, that Britain's failure to commit her reserve divisions to the continent and its decision to withdraw its fighters to Britain were but a precursor to the British signing of a separate peace with Hitler. Under these circumstances, Pétain believed it was best that France do its utmost to immediately come to terms with Germany.

In an attempt to allay that fear, British Gen. Sir Edward Spears, who had served as a liaison officer with the French during the Great War, traveled to Paris to meet personally with Pétain. The marshal received Spears warmly, and as the discussion turned to the fighting, Pétain walked him over to a wall map, where he had outlined the general dispositions of the French forces. Pétain's mood abruptly soured as he spoke of the impossible situation confronting the French army. There was no way the troops could hold, and he coldly stated that defeat was now inevitable. Pétain then became livid and angrily denounced "the leftist politicians and schoolteachers," whom he said were directly responsible for this defeat. He stated that their pacifist ideologies and failure to prepare the French people for war were at the heart of the military disaster unfolding at that moment, which he viewed as more a crisis of morale rather than as an actual battlefield defeat.

On June 5 the hammer fell as three German army groups began a series of superbly coordinated assaults, supported by powerful air strikes and the largest concentrations of German artillery thus encountered in the campaign. Weygand's defensive positions along the Somme-Aisne line sagged under the impact of the German attack. French soldiers fought heroically and, in fact, much to the surprise of the Germans, who considered the campaign already won, put up their stoutest resistance of the war. It was far too late, however, for by this stage they were badly outnumbered, had virtually no air cover or armor, and hence could not stand before a German army at the peak of its powers. After several days of the most intense fighting of the campaign, the Germans breached the Weygand Line and established bridgeheads across the Somme and the Aisne. The panzers rushed forward to exploit the breakthroughs, and as French resistance crumbled, the swift-moving armored formations destroyed any possibility for an orderly withdrawal.

A panic ensued as entire French divisions dissolved into mobs, intermingling with terrified civilian refugees fleeing the scene of battle. The roads south were choked with the detritus of defeat, and the Luftwaffe showed no mercy as it bombed and strafed the long columns heedless of civilian casualties. On June 10, Reynaud made the ominous decision to evacuate the French government from Paris to Bordeaux. The news stunned Parisians and an overwhelming, almost tangible, sense of defeat hung in the air over the suddenly silent capital.

At this moment of crisis, Reynaud led a delegation, which included Pétain, Weygand, and de Gaulle, to meet with British prime minister Winston Churchill on June 11, 1940. The mood was tense in the chateau where the meeting took place. Churchill took it on himself to put spirit into the French delegation, urging them to fortify Paris and make it the cornerstone of their defense. He turned to Pétain and reminded him of the dark days of March 1918, purposely flattering the marshal by giving him (rather than Foch) credit for rallying the Allied armies to victory and calling on him to do so again. Pétain replied that the present situation was completely different: in 1918 he had had sixty divisions in reserve and now there were none. In a pointed reference to the BEF's withdrawal from the current battle, he coolly noted that in 1918 the British had had sixty divisions as well and now they were gone too. Pétain believed that Britain had already abandoned France to the Germans.

Reynaud asked Churchill to commit every RAF squadron to the battle as this was the decisive moment of the campaign. Churchill refused, saying that the decisive moment would come when Hitler attacked Britain and that the RAF needed to be held back for that battle. "If we can keep command of the air, and if we can keep the seas open, we will win it all back for you." This did not reassure the French delegation.

Realizing that the British could not—or in the French view *would* not—commit any more forces to the fight, General Weygand stated that France may have to seek an armistice to preserve what was left of the nation and its army. Reynaud was furious at this remark and sharply informed his commanding general that an armistice was a political decision and thus not in Weygand's realm of responsibility. A sharp divide had been created within the Reynaud government between the premier and his military leaders regarding the further prosecution of the war. In the growing dispute, Pétain made no secret that he stood firmly with Weygand and others who advocated the signing of an armistice at the earliest possible date.

When the Allied conference resumed the next day, Churchill renewed his arguments for continued French resistance, including guerrilla warfare, arguing that the United States was bound to intervene in the near future. Reynaud was heartened by the reference to the United States, but Pétain and Weygand considered it unrealistic to rely on the Americans. By the time the meeting was over, it was clear to all where France was headed. As Churchill made his farewells he took aside the commander of the French navy, Admiral Darlan, and told him that whatever else occurred to make sure the French fleet did not fall into German hands. Darlan gave his solemn assurance that this would never happen. With that Churchill began pulling the small remnant of British forces left on the continent back to Great Britain, and on June 14, 1940, Paris fell to the Germans.

Reynaud rallied the dwindling support in his cabinet for the possibility of evacuating the government and what soldiers they could to the French colonies in North Africa to continue the struggle, but opposition to continuing the war had reached a crisis point. Both Weygand and Pétain began to openly advocate an armistice. The war was lost, they believed, and the time had come to save what was left of France and the army before it was too late. The Chamber of Deputies in Bordeaux began to champion the idea as well, and Reynaud felt the ground giving way beneath him. In this respect the deputies were merely doing what the elected representatives of a democracy were supposed to and that was to reflect the will of the people. By all estimations, the people of France desperately wanted peace and saw nothing to be gained by further resistance and indeed much to be lost in terms of additional territory, the overseas empire, and a longer and more difficult German occupation. Unable to rally his own government, Reynaud decided to resign rather than follow the odious policy of surrender advocated by the Chamber of Deputies and the high command. When he announced his resignation he requested, and the Chamber approved, that Marshal Pétain be asked to form a new government.

Why was Pétain chosen at this dire hour? He was the greatest living hero of France, a recognizable leader who had wide support from both the Left and the Right and was a man whom the people trusted and the army would follow. In fact, he was the only man in France who had such credentials. Also as a military man and hero of the Great War, it was believed that the Germans would respect Pétain more than a conventional French politician, and thus he would be able to get better terms from the enemy as well. The latter criteria would be hotly debated later, but it is clear that from the moment he assumed office Pétain believed the main task before him, and the one he had in fact been chosen to carry out, was the signing of an armistice with the Germans that would save the army and France. With that decided, any delay would be criminal as more French soldiers and civilians died every moment the war went on.

Immediately on assuming power, Pétain used his connections with Franco's government in Madrid to send out peace feelers to the Germans. On June 17, 1940, he went on national radio, for the first time as leader of France, to inform the French people that the war was over. The great hero, who had inspired an army and a nation with his defense of Verdun, now broadcast, "With a heavy heart I tell you today that it is necessary to stop the fighting."[4] It was the beginning of an ominous series of events that would destroy the brilliant reputation he had forged in decades of service to France.

There was little in the way of negotiations for the armistice. The French army was virtually destroyed, and the spirit of the French people to resist was broken. Alsace and Lorraine were transferred back to Germany, and Paris along with large swaths of French territory, including the entire Atlantic seaboard, fell under German occupation. France would have to pay reparations and make funds available to finance the German occupation of French territory. Still, Pétain's representative at the armistice talks managed to wring some concessions from the victor, including the retention of all French colonies and the French navy. Hitler, eager to end hostilities and avoid a prolongation of the conflict, over-ruled his generals and accepted these conditions. He also allowed for a section of southern France, soon to become infamous as Vichy France, to remain unoccupied by German forces and enjoy an ill-defined autonomy.

For Pétain, and indeed for most of France, World War II ended with the signing of the armistice with Germany on June 25, 1940. France was defeated, and it was widely believed in France and elsewhere that Britain would have to make peace as well. It was assumed that a formal peace treaty would be signed in the near future, and however harsh the terms, the Germans would at least go home after that and the process of rebuilding France would begin.

To the astonishment of many, Britain refused to capitulate. Winston Churchill rebuffed all openings for a diplomatic solution to the conflict and instead braced his people for a long struggle against the Germans. Ever since the evacuation at Dunkirk and the RAF's withdrawal from the continent, the French had felt abandoned by their ally. Many in France saw Churchill's obstinate refusal to discuss terms as one more way in which France was made to suffer for British policy and believed that the sooner the British came to their senses the quicker France's ordeal would end. Yet the ordeal was in fact just beginning.

As Britain braced itself for the German onslaught the issue of the French navy became foremost in Churchill's mind. The German Kriegsmarine lacked the vessels for a blockade or amphibious invasion of Britain. However, the Italian fleet was at the Germans' disposal, and with it the Axis powers could mount a challenge to the Royal Navy. If the Germans could somehow acquire the French navy, which included some of the most powerful warships in the world, they might gain a decisive advantage in the coming struggle. The thought of the French navy falling into German hands was a nightmare scenario for Churchill. A combined force of German, Italian, and French warships might be able to wrest control of the English Channel and allow for an invasion of Britain.

The only warships still under the direct control of Pétain's new government, and therefore theoretically vulnerable to German seizure, were a scattered number of cruisers and destroyers in Toulon and Algeria, the battleship *Richelieu* at Dakar in French West Africa, and a powerful squadron, consisting of two battleships, two battle cruisers, and thirteen destroyers, under Adm. Marcel Gensoul's command at Mers-el-Kébir in Algeria.

Although approximately half the French navy was already at British bases, Churchill became fixated on Gensoul's squadron and determined to make sure that these remaining ships did not fall into German hands. Consequently, he ordered V. Adm. Sir James Sommerville to demand the surrender of Admiral Gensoul's squadron in Algeria and, if that ultimatum was refused, to destroy the French squadron. On July 3, 1940, after brief and unsuccessful negotiations, British battleships and battle cruisers attacked the French warships in Mers-el-Kébir. The French vessels had been partially disarmed by the terms of the armistice, were not ready for action, and never had a chance. The French battleships *Dunkerque* and *Bretagne* took heavy damage and then ran aground when they attempted to escape. As *Bretagne* struggled to get free a heavy-caliber shell penetrated her ammunition magazine, and she exploded in a thunderous ball of fire. A small number of French ships miraculously escaped the British onslaught, but as darkness fell over Mers-el-Kébir the harbor was lit by the flames of the naval might of France burning from the attack by her erstwhile ally. The following day British aircraft launched air strikes on the defenseless *Dunkerque*, still stuck fast on a sandbar, taking the lives of yet more Frenchmen. By the time the attacks were over, 1,297 French sailors had been killed, and another 354 were wounded. The British had suffered only slight damage without a single fatality.

Simultaneous with their attack on Mers-el-Kébir British soldiers and marines stormed aboard French warships anchored in Plymouth and Portsmouth, seized control of the vessels, and imprisoned their crews. The Royal Navy also interned the battleship *Lorraine* and its escort vessels in Alexandria, and a few days later British aircraft bombed and damaged the French battleship *Richelieu* at anchor in Dakar on the west coast of Africa.

The reaction in France to these British attacks was one of shock, followed by a virulent outburst of anger toward Britain. Admiral Darlan was particularly incensed at the British action and ordered French warships in the Mediterranean to sortie and attempt to intercept Sommeville's squadron and attack British merchant shipping. But Pétain remained a moderate voice. He cancelled Darlan's orders to attack British shipping and authorized only a symbolic "bombing" (the planes purposely dropped their bombs in the sea) of Gibraltar as a form of protest to British actions. Nevertheless, he broke diplomatic relations with Britain and issued a statement to the people of France explaining the reasons for his action:

> England, breaking a long alliance, has attacked unexpectedly and has destroyed French ships immobilized in port and partially disarmed. Nothing foreshadowed such an aggression. Nothing justifies it. Did the British government believe that we would deliver our warships to the Italians and the Germans? If it believed such a thing, it was wrong.[5]

The scheming French politician Pierre Laval used the British attack as the basis for a series of bold moves. Acting in Pétain's name, although not always in consultation with the marshal, he began to gather support among the exiled members of the Chamber of Deputies for a complete overhaul of the government. With their nation's armed forces defeated, their country under occupation, and their former ally having viciously destroyed the last remnants of their power, the people of France were desperate for a savior. The time had come, Laval argued, to rally the nation around the one man who could lead France through this dark time, Marshal Philippe Pétain.

Pétain initially viewed his role as political leader of France as a temporary expedient to secure a peace and end the war before all of France was destroyed. Yet now his ego was stroked by the idea of being a leader of an actual national revival, soon to be dubbed the "National Revolution." He longed to take an active part in remaking France in his image and ridding the nation of the past twenty years of socialist and Marxist teachings and programs whose bitter fruit had been the defeat of 1940. France would be strong again, France would be great again, and it was his duty to make that come to pass. The Chamber of Deputies voted overwhelmingly to name him head of state, and he accepted his new office. At this point he began to use the soon to be familiar phrase, "We, Philippe Pétain, Marshal of France . . . " as the preamble to a host of decrees that would remake society in Vichy France. The far-right Action Française became a dominant force in the new chamber, and with the party's support Pétain began to create a French fascist regime.

Pétain had been intrigued by fascism since his first encounter with it in Spain. The events of the Spanish Civil War and the first two years of World War II lent further credence to his notion that fascism was the wave of the future. It exalted the spirit of sacrifice for the nation, instead of the slothful pursuit of pleasure and money that capitalism had offered. It also rejected the atheism and internationalism of communism in favor of a nationalism founded on the traditional pillars of French society. The phrase *Liberté, Egalité, Fraternité* (liberty, equality, fraternity), which had been the mantra of French republicanism since the days of the Revolution, was now replaced with the fascist call words *Travail, Famille, Patrie* (work, family, fatherland).

The remaking of French society included a new law known as the *Statut des Juifs* introduced by the far-right members of the chamber. Formally approved on October 3, 1940, this new law prevented Jews from holding elected office in Vichy France and excluded them from being lawyers, judges, schoolteachers, and soldiers. To his immense discredit Pétain approved of this measure, although he amended the law to provide exceptions to Jews who had served in World War I or who came from families of long-proven loyalty to France.

Anti-Semitism in Vichy was based largely on the conspiratorial theories of the far Right, which believed that Jews represented a secret society in France whose loyalty was to their group rather than the nation. Thus, unlike the Nazis' racially motivated anti-Semitism, Vichy's fascist ideology was fueled by nationalism and the desire to exclude those who refused to assimilate into French society. Pétain personally was no more, and no less, anti-Semitic than any other French person. However, he did believe that Jews were part of the problem of the Third Republic's chaotic democracy and that they needed to be controlled just as the Free Masons and communists who viewed themselves independent of the France they were ostensibly part of. While different than Hitler's National Socialist regime, Vichy's policy played into the hands of the

Nazis, who occupied the bulk of France and who would eventually implement far darker policies of their own against Jews and other ethnic minorities in occupied Europe.

Meanwhile, overseas the British refused to accept Vichy as France's legitimate government and did not respect Pétain's view of his country's status as a neutral. Supported by Britain, Gen. Charles de Gaulle began to rally the vast overseas holdings of France to the cause of "Fighting France." He made nightly radio broadcasts from London condemning Pétain's regime and calling for French people everywhere to rise and join him in continuing the war against Germany. French colonies, beginning with Chandernagor in India, started to rise against Vichy and join de Gaulle's cause. August 26 to 28, 1940, became the "Three Glorious Days," as Chad, the Cameroons, and the Congo all declared for de Gaulle. Suddenly the general was no longer a lone voice but a recognized leader of a sprawling African empire. Churchill was thrilled with de Gaulle's progress and was determined to make full use of this momentum to capture all French possessions in sub-Saharan Africa for the Free French cause.

In August 1940 a British naval squadron under Admiral Cunningham transported de Gaulle and two thousand of his soldiers to Dakar, West Africa, with the hope that the mere presence of the Frenchman and clever propaganda would cause the colony to rise and join the Free French cause. Unfortunately, this was not the case. After the British air raids on Dakar in July, Pétain had sent reinforcements under Gen. Pierre Boisson to the strategic base with orders to fortify it and resist further Gaullist inroads into France's African empire. Boisson recognized Pétain as the head of France's legitimate government and saw de Gaulle as nothing more than a dangerous renegade. Thus, whatever happened Boisson was determined to fight and defend his position.

The Anglo-Gaullist operation began with British aircraft dropping leaflets all over the city asking the citizens to rise and join the Free French while de Gaulle broadcast the same message over radio and loudspeakers. The small disturbances caused by these efforts were swiftly put down by Boisson, who also rejected de Gaulle's personal entreaties toward him. The Gaullists' attempt to negotiate under a white flag resulted in an exchange of gunfire, and from that point forward a real battle was on. Resistance was too fierce to attempt a landing with de Gaulle's small force, and after consulting with Admiral Cunningham, the Free French leader agreed that it was necessary to withdraw. The incident at Dakar demonstrated that de Gaulle was not the universal symbol of defiant France that he aspired to be and that many French citizens were loyal to Pétain. In fact the British, and later the Americans, constantly searched for alternatives to de Gaulle, though they never successfully found one who could match him in appeal.

The engagement at Dakar inaugurated an undeclared war between Britain and Vichy, and a civil war between Vichy France and the Free French movement. This war would spread across Africa and the Middle East as one Vichy-controlled colony after another was captured by the British with Free French assistance.

The Gaullists viewed those who were loyal to Vichy as traitors in collusion with the hated Germans. For its part, the Vichy government believed the Gaullists to be mercenaries bought and paid for by the treacherous British, whose hands were stained with the blood of Mers-el-Kébir. Pétain viewed the Free French as de Gaulle direct challenge to his Vichy regime. In Pétain's view the "civil war" inaugurated by de Gaulle and his British masters brought only needless hardship to a French nation and people desperate for peace. He declared de Gaulle a traitor and condemned him to death in absentia.

The complete collapse of Anglo-French relations, the establishment of a French fascist regime in Vichy, and the entreaties of the increasingly powerful Germanophile Pierre Laval made Hitler think that France could perhaps become a useful ally in the war against Britain. When FM Hermann Göring's Luftwaffe failed to bomb Britain into submission in the fall of 1940, Hitler began to think of alternative ways of securing his western flank. With his attention already turned back to his long sought- for *Drang nach Osten*, Hitler hoped to keep the British busy in the Mediterranean and elsewhere with a minimal commitment of German forces. To this end Hitler sought a meeting with the new dictator of France, Pétain.

Pétain agreed to meet the German chancellor as he believed the only way a permanent peace could be secured and the rebuilding of France could commence was for the two leaders to discuss their differences face to face and work out an agreement. From Laval, who was in constant contact with the Germans, he deduced that Hitler was planning to put pressure on Spain as well as France to join the war as allies of Germany. Laval was excited by the idea, but this was not what Pétain wanted. In fact he believed that such a move would be disastrous for France, and unlike Laval, Pétain loathed the Germans. Hitler was riding high on a crest of success and stood at the peak of his power and at the head of the most dangerously powerful regime in world history, yet Pétain had determined to resist him.

On October 24, 1940, Pétain journeyed to his meeting with the leader of the nation that had destroyed France. He was eager to meet with Hitler and thought that the German chancellor could be reasoned with on the important issues that needed to be settled. In fact, it would be a defining moment for Pétain and his Vichy regime, forever tainting them with the stain of collaboration and treason. The tragic irony that this meeting occurred on the twenty-fourth anniversary of the recapture of Fort Douaumont during the Battle of Verdun was probably lost on those in attendance.

When Hitler saw Marshal Pétain, he broke free of his entourage with a swift stride, and as the flashbulbs of the German and French media popped, he enthusiastically reached forward to shake Pétain's hand, stating as he did so, "It is a pleasure to meet a Frenchman who bears no responsibility for this war."[6]

The two men and their respective entourages moved to a meeting room, and pleasantries were swiftly put aside as the real business at hand began. Based on previous conversations with Laval, Hitler had expected a spirit of cooperation with Pétain, and thus he became increasingly angry with the marshal's cold reticence. This was not what Hitler had anticipated, and his voice rose as he said, "If France will not defend herself and still has sympathy for England, she will lose her colonial empire at the end of the war and be subjected to peace terms as onerous as England's." Pétain's face darkened, and he replied that no peace of reprisal had ever lasted in history. Hitler's frustration mounted as he told Pétain he did not want a peace of reprisal. He wanted peace for all of Europe, but Britain stood in the way. Therefore, Hitler declared, "I cannot bring about peace until France makes up its mind to help me defeat the British."[7]

Pétain responded by asking Hitler, as the first step to a peace process between the two nations, to immediately release all French soldiers held as prisoners of war. Hitler refused, stating no prisoners could be released until the war was over. Since Britain continued to resist, Germany must not only retain the French prisoners but also make use of captured territory in France to further prosecute the war until the British accepted defeat. Hitler told Pétain that he would guarantee the integrity of the French empire overseas and that Germany would reward its friends at the time of the final victory, perhaps, he implied, with British colonies in Africa. However, Hitler warned, this was only possible if France formally broke with Britain and became Germany's ally. Pétain refused. He told Hitler that France was a defeated nation and desired only peace.

Pétain asked that the costs of the occupation foisted upon a defeated France be lessened and that steps be taken to open up the border between France's occupied and unoccupied zones. Hitler said he would take these issues and all of the other points Pétain had raised under consideration provided that France acted in a spirit of collaboration with Germany. He emphasized that French actions in this regard would heavily influence his decisions on the matters of the return of prisoners and territory to France. Pétain agreed to this and offered to make a formal statement to the French people urging them to collaborate with the Germans, although again he insisted that such measures would not include military cooperation.

At the end of the Montoire meeting, Pétain had gained only vague assurances of rewards for good behavior and promises of future talks with Germany. He had not lost anything, however, and he had formally rebuffed any notion of France becoming the Germans' ally. If those appear to be mild accomplishments, it must be remembered that Pétain was at the head of a defeated nation. French territory was occupied and its military forces were shattered. The marshal had virtually nothing to bargain with. By way of contrast, Premier Edouard Daladier and Prime Minister Neville Chamberlain had achieved far less in their negotiations with Hitler at Munich in 1938, when they represented two of the most powerful nations on Earth.

For his part, Hitler was bitterly disappointed with the Montoire meeting. He had hoped that a fascist France would become a military ally of Germany that would bolster his western defenses and be a tremendous assistance in the war against Britain and in his future war against communism in the east. But in fact Pétain had icily rejected even his most basic of military requests.

Whatever victory Pétain had won in rejecting Hitler's proposal for a Franco-German alliance, he swiftly squandered it in the speech he made to the French people. "I enter into the way of collaboration," he announced. With Hitler's vague assurances for better treatment in mind, he stated that many benefits would come to the French people through a peaceful collaboration with the occupying Germans, including the early release of French prisoners of war, a lightening of war reparations, and more autonomy. Such things would be granted, however, only if the French made their good intentions toward the Germans known and did not cause trouble for the occupying power.[8]

The term "collaboration" soon took on a sinister connotation as Vichy authorities went to extraordinary lengths to please their German masters, for example, by deporting foreign Jews from French territory to the Nazi concentration camps where most of them would perish. "Collaboration" also meant failure to resist Nazi programs for conscripting young Frenchmen from the occupied zone into forced labor battalions and the use of French industry to manufacture war matériel for the German military. Pétain's collaborationist policies did not win the release of a single French prisoner of war. Instead the Nazis ruthlessly exploited the obvious concern the old marshal had for his captive troops to blackmail and coerce him into following their requests. Pétain was forever reminded by the Germans that it was but a short train ride from a prisoner of war camp to a concentration camp, and the marshal was to be held personally responsible for such a fate befalling these one million men if his behavior did not conform to Hitler's requests.

Pétain truly believed he was the ruler of a neutral and sovereign nation, but the cold hard truth was that the rump state of Vichy existed only at the pleasure of Pétain's Nazi masters. His reputation as a man whose patriotism was beyond question was also exploited by the Germans to help maintain order among the French people.

The charade of Vichy independence was shattered in November 1942 when Anglo-American forces launched Operation Torch, the invasion of French North Africa. The North African colonies had remained under Vichy control after 1940 and secured the rear of the Axis forces in their campaign against the British. As Field Marshal Rommel's vaunted Afrika Korps fought to a standstill in Egypt, Anglo-American forces planned for a full-scale invasion of French North Africa to flank Rommel and drive the Axis powers back across the Mediterranean. As the time for the landings neared, Prime Minister Churchill and President Roosevelt still held out hope that whatever Pétain's shortcomings, he was not pro-German. His actions up to this point could be explained as those of a man made helpless by the horrendous circumstances his country had fallen into. Both Allies believed there was still time for Pétain to redeem himself and his Vichy regime.

On November 8, 1942, Anglo-American forces began landing in Morocco and Algeria. Pinckney Tuck, the American chargé d'affaires to the Vichy government, visited Pétain to inform him of the news. Pétain greeted the American and announced that he was "deeply grieved" by the news of the landings and this violation of French sovereignty. Much to the disappointment of all concerned, Pétain's official response to Operation Torch was, "We are attacked. We defend ourselves. . . . It is French honor that is at stake."[9]

In spite of the official rebuff, Roosevelt and Churchill persisted in their negotiations with Vichy authorities in North Africa, including Admiral Darlan and General Juin, and indirectly with Pétain's government. Through a combination of skillful diplomacy and threats, fighting between Vichy forces and Anglo-American troops was kept to a minimum.

During these tense negotiations pressure was building on Pétain from all sides. Laval and his pro-German clique were clamoring for Vichy to declare war on the United States and Great Britain while a small handful of his personal aides argued that the time had come to declare for the Allies. To make matters worse, Hitler had announced that Vichy could no longer be neutral and that it must declare itself an ally of Germany's or be considered an enemy. Pétain was clearly overwhelmed by the pressure of the moment. At eighty-six years old his faculties had visibly declined, and he appeared benumbed by the situation's gravity. While others argued and negotiated, Pétain did nothing. On November 11, Vichy forces in Morocco defied Pétain's edict to resist and laid down their arms. Some believed that at this time Pétain was playing a double game with the Germans until he could safely make his next move. There was a belief that, especially now that his old friends the Americans were in the fight, he would lead France to the side of her liberators.

This notion was reinforced when Pétain's representative in North Africa, Admiral Darlan, was recognized by the British and Americans as "representing French interests in North Africa." Darlan announced he had reached an agreement with the American authorities, purposely refusing to mention the British, and would defend North Africa along-side the Americans. Pétain was stunned by Darlan's defection, yet others saw it as an opportunity. Pétain's closest aide, Bernard Serrigny, told the marshal to immediately go to North Africa with all the military force he could muster, including the remnants of the French fleet and air force and join with Darlan and the Allies. Whatever his past mistakes, whatever his policies, there was still time for redemption, and this was his moment. No, Pétain told Serrigny, it was not possible.

Hitler reacted to the deteriorating situation in Vichy and the North African colonies by delivering an ultimatum to Pétain. There could no longer be any question of French neutrality, Hitler said. Pétain's regime must declare itself to be a member of the Axis powers and join the war as a German ally or suffer the consequences. Pétain steadfastly refused to join with Hitler, and as a result German troops invaded and occupied Vichy France at the end of November 1942. The illusion of French autonomy under the marshal disappeared. From this point forward German guards became a permanent presence with Pétain, and the Gestapo monitored his every move and pronouncement. Pétain was now simply a pawn in the hands of his Nazi masters.

His years were also catching up with him. He routinely fell asleep during cabinet meetings and often appeared confused by events and people visiting him. Senility had begun to take its unrelenting grip on the octogenarian marshal, and his mind and body became feebler than ever. While at times he displayed a coherent intellect, these episodes were the exception, and during the final two years of his regime he increasingly lost touch with the world around him. Pétain remained a figurehead and a symbol of an essentially defunct Vichy regime from 1942 to 1944, during which time he retained a remarkable degree of popularity with the bulk of the French population. Many in France believed Pétain was a buffer between the Nazi occupation forces and the French people and offered a more reasonable solution to the situation than the radical tactics of the communist-inspired Resistance.

Pétain was horrified by the emergence of the Resistance after Hitler invaded the Soviet Union in 1941. He was deeply concerned that the group's actions would bring terrible retribution from the Germans, who would exact their revenge on the innocent millions of French men and women living under their heel. He was also appalled by the Resistance's politics, which were overwhelmingly leftist. Pétain viewed the Maquis as a force for anarchy and communist revolution that threatened his own regime and the peace and stability of France itself. He therefore took the extraordinary step of authorizing military action against the Resistance. In 1943 he authorized the transformation of the *Service d'ordre légionnaire*, a right-wing militia group, into the *Milice*. Led by Gen. Joseph Darnand, the Milice were charged with hunting down and destroying Resistance forces in France.

Darnand was seduced by the dark ideas of fascism and Nazism, and his Milice received considerable assistance from the Gestapo. His methods were brutal, and torture and summary executions were routinely used against suspected members of the Resistance. Pétain believed the Milice were a necessary evil to combat the radical Left, but even he became appalled at Darnand's methods and his open collusion with the Gestapo. He reprimanded Darnand and told him to reform his methods and restrain his men. Darnand sarcastically responded that Pétain had authorized his every action and that he was merely performing the unsavory tasks that the marshal could not carry out himself. Pétain did not support Darnand after that, but he did nothing to restrain him either and the torture and killings continued unabated.

In June 1944 the Allies landed in Normandy, and their forces included a sizable contingent of Free French troops. They had come to liberate France, but Pétain, with his Gestapo guards by his side, denounced the landings as an "invasion" and urged all French men and women to resist the Allied forces. These appeals fell on deaf ears as, for the first time since 1940, Pétain's hold over the French people was broken. Cheering crowds greeted General de Gaulle and the other leaders of the Free French forces. De Gaulle declared that he was the head of the new Provisional Government of the French Republic (GPRF) and denounced Pétain's Vichy regime as an illegitimate puppet state of the Nazis.

As Allied forces pushed through France, the Germans urged Pétain to go to Germany to ensure his "safety." Pétain refused and so as Allied forces prepared to enter Paris, the Gestapo arrested Pétain, as well as his pro-German minister Laval and other members of the Vichy government, and forcibly removed them to Sigmaringen, Germany. There Pétain and his ministers remained as a "government in exile" until they were captured by Free French forces in April 1945.

With little debate the provisional government of France decided to try Marshal Pétain and other leaders of Vichy France for treason. The trial began on July 23, 1945, amid a media circus and a throng of thousands of Frenchmen who came to see not only Pétain but the French government itself tried for its actions during the most horrendous episode in the nation's history. The trial was a national sensation, and it seemed as if the French were conducting a form of exorcism to rid themselves of the demons of Nazi collaboration.

Pétain appeared in the courtroom attired in a simple khaki uniform bearing the seven-star insignia of a French marshal. Of his many medals, he wore only the *Médaille Militaire* awarded him for bravery under fire during World War I. He was now eighty-nine years old and was accompanied by his personal physician and a team of nurses. His hands trembled uncontrollably and his eyes seemed to lack focus as the High Court prosecutor read out the long list of charges against him. The charges were serious: collusion with the enemy, persecution of Jews, persecution of communists and other political groups, destruction of the republic and erection of a fascist state in its place, collaboration with the German invaders, supplying war matériel to the Germans, and sanctioning the use of military force against members of the Resistance. The list ran on and on. The crimes of Vichy were now laid at the feet of the man who had been the leader of that regime. Figurehead or no, he would answer for it all.

As the prosecutor began his questioning, Pétain abruptly rose from his seat, holding a sheaf of papers in his trembling hands. He addressed the court in a firm and clear voice that seemed to belie his apparent physical frailty.

> History will show the evils from which I saved France. . . . Each day, with a dagger at my throat, I had to battle the demands of the enemy. . . . I surrendered nothing essential. . . . My actions sustained France. I assured France of *la vie et le pain* [life and bread]. . . . I prepared the road to liberation. . . . The people of France . . . conferred power upon me. It is to them only that I am responsible.[10]

As the courtroom exploded into shouting and denunciations, the marshal slumped back into his chair. There he remained, silent and dignified, through the remainder of the trial.

The witnesses for the prosecution were as illustrious as they were numerous and included former premiers Paul Reynaud and Edouard Daladier. As the trial progressed it became clear to many observers that whatever Pétain's shortcomings, he was really being tried for the failures of France itself in 1940, and they believed the old marshal was being made a scapegoat for others.

Some observers were less than pleased with how the High Court conducted the trial. Charles de Gaulle believed the court focused far too much on "political" subjects such as Vichy's anti-Semitic laws and persecution of communists. He believed the court needed to address the decision by Pétain's government to conclude an armistice with the Germans while French soldiers were still fighting in the field and while France, through its empire, still had the ability to resist the invader. "The faults of Vichy," de Gaulle concluded, "all flowed inevitably from this poisoned spring."

As for laying the blame for all the bad decisions of 1940 and the crimes of Vichy on Pétain, de Gaulle believed this was a mistake. He thought, and many concurred, that the real crimes were committed by those like Laval who had performed despicable actions in the name of the marshal. He later wrote, "The facts cited, the testimonies given . . . made it clear that his had been the drama of a [senile man] lacking the strength necessary to lead men and control events."[11]

Nevertheless, Pétain symbolized Vichy and thus it was clear from the beginning where the trial would lead and there was little speculation as to the verdict, though some about the sentencing. At the end of the defense counsel's presentation, Pétain spoke for the first time since the opening of the proceedings. In his final statement to the court he said, "Deal with me according to your consciences. Mine brings me no reproach, since during a life that has already been long, and having arrived at the threshold of death, I affirm that I have had no other ambition than to serve France."[12]

On August 15, 1945, Pétain was pronounced guilty of all charges and condemned to death. The court, however, recommended leniency, and de Gaulle took this opportunity to intervene. Citing Marshal Pétain's heroic service in the Great War and his advanced years, de Gaulle ordered the death sentence be commuted to life imprisonment. After a brief stay at a military prison in the Pyrenees, Pétain was transported to the Île d'Yeu off France's west coast. His wife, Eugénie, accompanied him into exile and was a constant visitor to his cell. He languished there until death finally came for him at age ninety-five on July 23, 1951.

Over the course of his long life Pétain had long envisioned where he wanted to be buried. The resting place Pétain sought was in the midst of his soldiers and it was his dying wish to be buried on the battlefield of Verdun, at the ossuaire near the battered remnants of Fort Douaumont, surrounded by the graves of his men who had fallen in the great battle. However, this was not to be.

Pétain's devoted lawyer Jacques Isorni petitioned to have the marshal buried at Verdun, but the French government rejected this appeal. Protests erupted throughout France in reaction to the decision, but the government held firm and insisted that such a burial was politically impossible as it would be tantamount to a general pardon for the marshal's actions as head of Vichy. Thus, it was decreed that Pétain would be buried on the Île d'Yeu, remaining in exile even after death.

The government also insisted that Pétain not be buried in his uniform, but Eugénie flaunted this decree and personally dressed the marshal's body herself in his French army uniform and pinned his treasured Médaille Militaire to his chest. The local authorities did their best to keep the funeral low-key, but Verdun veterans clamored to be allowed onto the island to take part. The funeral procession eventually numbered approximately seven thousand people. Eight Verdun veterans and two former prisoners of war from World War II served as the pall bearers.

Pétain was a man who lived too long. Had he died before World War II, like Foch and Joffre, he would today be remembered as one of France's greatest heroes. His military talents and leadership skills shone forth during the Great War, and his compassion for his soldiers and their trials made him the most beloved of all French generals of that conflict. Yet he did live, and while it is critical to appreciate the man he was, it is also important to know the man he became. With his nation and its army shattered, he did what he thought best to help each of them, but in the end failed them both miserably. Today Marshal Philippe Pétain's mortal remains still lay entombed on his island prison, and all efforts to move them have failed. Yet wherever his body's final resting place is located, his spirit will always be with his beloved soldiers of Verdun.

Notes

Chapter 1
1. Guy Pedroncini, *Pétain: Le Soldat, 1914–1940* (Paris: Perrin, 1998), 18.
2. J-R Tourneaux, *Pétain and De Gaulle* (London: Heinemann, 1966), 23.

Chapter 2
1. Pedroncini, *Pétain: Le Soldat*, 78.
2. Robert A. Doughty, *Pyrrhic Victory: French Strategy and Operations in the Great War* (Cambridge, MA: Belknap Press, 2005), 172.
3. Stephen Ryan, *Pétain the Soldier* (South Brunswick, NJ: A. S. Barnes, 1969), 70.
4. Rapport du Général Pétain, 1er Novembre 1915, cited in Barthélemy Palat, *La Grande Guerre sur le Front Occidental* (Paris: Berger-Levrault, 1922), 9:577–578.

Chapter 3
1. Erich von Falkenhayn, *General Headquarters 1914–1916 and Its Critical Decisions* (London: Hutchison, 1919; Nashville, TN: Battery Press, 2000), 217–218. Citations are to the Battery Press edition.
2. Henri Ortholan, *Le Général Séré de Rivières: Le Vauban de la Revanche* (Paris: Bernard Giovanangeli Éditeur, 2003); and Guy Le Hallé, *Le Système Séré de Rivières* (Louviers Cedex: Ysec Éditions, 2001).
3. Philippe Pétain, *Verdun* (New York: Dial Press, 1930), 222–23.
4. Ibid., 78.

5. Ibid., 93.

6. Jean-Pierre Turbergue, ed., *Les 300 Jours de Verdun* (Triel-sur-Seine: Éditions Italiques, 2006), 117.

7. Pétain, *Verdun*, 122–23.

8. Sylvain-Eugène Raynal, *Le Drame du Ft. Vaux* (Verdun: Éditions Lorraines, 1927).

9. Les Armées Françaises dans la Grande Guerre, Tome 4: *Verdun et la Somme*, Troisième Volume Bataille de la Somme (fin), Offensives françaises à Verdun (3 septembre–fin décembre 1916), 321 (hereafter cited as AFGG).

10. II Armée, État-Major, Artillerie, 30 octobre 1916, "Note sur les tirs exécutés sur les routes, pistes, bivouacs, abris, villages, gares, etc., pendant les combats du 20–25 octobre 1916," Service Historique de l'Armée de Terre, Archives de la Guerre, Château de Vincennes, Vincennes, France, 19 N 430 (hereafter cited as SHAT).

11. Joseph Joffre, *The Personal Memoirs of Joffre* (New York: Harper and Brothers, 1932), 2:494–495.

12. Erich Ludendorff, *Ludendorff's Own Story* (New York: Harper and Brothers, 1920), 1:344.

13. AFGG, Tome 4, 3:420.

14. Ludendorff, *Ludendorff's Own Story*, 1:345.

15. Frank H. Simonds, *History of the World War* (Garden City, NY: Doubleday & Page, 1919), 3:192.

16. Joffre, *Personal Memoirs of Joffre*, 450.

Chapter 4

1. Palat, *La Grande Guerre sur le Front Occidental*, 12:163–68.

2. Richard M. Watt, *Dare Call It Treason* (New York: Simon & Schuster, 1963), 169.

3. AFGG, Tome 5 (Paris: Imprimerie Nationale, 1922–39), 1: 689–712.

4. Guy Pedroncini, *Les Mutineries de 1917* (Paris: Presses Universitaires de France, 1967), 181–278; and Jean-Baptiste Duroselle, *La Grande Guerre des Français, 1914–1918* (Paris: Perrin, 1998), 203.

5. Charles de Gaulle, *France and Her Army* (London: Hutchinson, 1945), 103.

6. Général Laure, *Le Commandement en Chef des Armées Françaises: Du 15 Mai 1917 à L'Armistice* (Paris: Éditions Berger-Levrault, 1937), 8; and Pedroncini, *Pétain: Le Soldat*, 170–181.

7. Georges Clemenceau, *The Grandeur and Misery of Victory* (New York: Harcourt, Brace, 1930), 38–39.

8. Jean de Pierrefeu, *Inside French Headquarters, 1915–1918* (London: Geoffrey Bles, 1924), 269.

9. John J. Pershing, *My Experiences in the First World War* (New York: Da Capo, 1995), 1: 364–365.

10. Final Report of Gen. John J. Pershing, September 1, 1919, *The United States Army in the World War* (Washington, DC: GPO, 1948), 12:140 (hereafter cited as USAWW); and Pershing, *My Experiences*, 2:84.

11. "Preparation d'actions offensives entre Aisne et Marne, 14 juin–12 juillet [1918]," 400-30.9, RG 165 U.S. National Archives and Records Administration; and Guy Pedroncini, *Pétain: Général en Chef, 1917–1918*, 2nd ed. (Paris: Presses Universitaires de France, 1997), 380.

12. GQG Armées Nord et du Nord-Est, "Note sur le Moral des Troupes d'après le Contrôle Postal pendant la Period du 22 Juin au 3 Juillet 1918," SHAT, 16 N 1485.

13. Pedroncini, *Pétain: Le Soldat*, 381–382; and Laure, *Commandement en Chef*, 106–107.

14. Ferdinand Foch, telephone message to Philippe Pétain, July 15, 1918, in USAWW, 5:242.

15. Joseph Hellé and Berdoulat, "The A.E.F. in Their First Great Offensive," in *As They Saw Us* (Garden City, NY: Doubleday, Doran, 1929), 156.

16. War Diary, Army Group German Crown Prince, July 18, 1918, and Army Group German Crown Prince, Morning Reports, July 19, 1918, in General Service Schools, *The German Offensive of July 15, 1918: Marne Source Book* (Ft. Leavenworth, KS: General Service Schools Press, 1923), 621–624.

17. Paul von Hindenburg, *Out of My Life* (London: Cassell, 1920), 386.

18. Crown Prince Wilhelm, *Memoirs of the Crown Prince of Germany* (New York: Charles Scribner's Sons, 1922), 191, 237, 240.

Chapter 5

1. Pétain, *Verdun*, 213–214.
2. Ibid., 234.
3. Pedroncini, *Pétain: Le Soldat*, 423–452.
4. Herbert R. Lottman, *Pétain: Hero or Traitor?* (New York: Viking, 1985), 131.

Chapter 6

1. Pierre Héring, *La Vie Exemplaire de Philippe Pétain* (Paris: Paris-Livres, 1956), 77.
2. William Shirer, *The Collapse of the Third Republic: An Inquiry Into the Fall of France in 1940* (New York: Simon & Schuster, 1969), 699.
3. Paul Baudouin, *The Private Diaries of Paul Baudouin* (London: Eyre & Spottiswoode, 1948), 57.
4. Shirer, *Collapse of the Third Republic*, 854.
5. Sisley Huddleston, *Pétain: Patriot or Traitor?* (London: Andrew Dakers, 1951), 69.
6. Robert Aron, *The Vichy Regime, 1940–1944* (Boston: Beacon Press, 1969), 218.
7. Ibid., 219.
8. Robert O. Paxton, *Vichy France: Old Guard and New Order, 1940–1944* (New York: Columbia University Press, 1972), 77.
9. Charles Williams, *Pétain* (London: Little, Brown, 2005), 421.
10. *Time Magazine*, August 6, 1945.
11. Charles de Gaulle, *The Complete War Memoirs of Charles de Gaulle* (New York: Carroll & Graf, 1998), 951–952.
12. Williams, *Pétain*, 510.

Bibliographic Essay

Although Pétain never wrote a memoir, his book *Verdun* (New York: Dial Press, 1930) comes close to being autobiographical in places and is a necessary starting point for understanding the battle that defined Pétain, his army, and France in the twentieth century. Although in the main the book is a straightforward narrative, Pétain's sympathy for the French soldiers' plight and the ordeal they endured at Verdun is given special attention. The book remains the essential starting point for any serious study of the Battle of Verdun.

Another important work by Pétain is his account of the French army mutinies of 1917 titled "A Crisis of Morale in the French Nation at War." The manuscript was given to British liaison officer Gen. Sir Edward Spears, who translated and published the full text in his book *Two Men Who Saved France: Pétain and De Gaulle* (New York: Stein and Day, 1966). The essay is crucial to understanding the mutinies and Pétain's role in rallying the French army in this dark moment.

The main primary sources for information on Pétain's military career are works by his aides. Bernard Serrigny's *Trente Ans avec Pétain* (Paris: Plon, 1959) is a lively and informative read, heavily laced with personal anecdotes. While certainly admiring of his chief, Serrigny also attempts to maintain a balanced coverage of his subject. General Laure's *Pétain* (Paris: Berger-Levrault, 1941) and Jean de Pierrefeu's *Inside French Headquarters, 1915–1918* (London: Geoffrey Bles, 1924) also provide wonderful firsthand observations of Pétain as a military commander.

Biographies of Pétain by historians abound, and he is easily the most written about French commander of World War I. While the number of biographies about him dwarfs those of his peers Joffre or Foch, the statistic is a bit misleading as the overwhelming majority of these biographers pay scant attention to Pétain's life and career from 1856 to 1939 and instead focus almost exclusively on his leadership of Vichy France in World War II.

There are a few exceptions to this rule, however, including two superb biographies of Pétain available in English. Stephen Ryan's *Pétain the Soldier* (South Brunswick, NJ: A. S. Barnes, 1969) is a wonderfully written and enlightening book filled with astute observations and insights on Pétain's military career and philosophy of war. Charles Williams's *Pétain* (London: Little, Brown, 2005) is an excellent book that provides a sound and balanced examination of the marshal's life and is especially useful for insights into his personal life.

Pétain's greatest biographer is Guy Pedroncini, who has written several books on Pétain and various aspects of his career. His monumental *Pétain: Le Soldat, 1914–1940* (Paris: Perrin, 1998) is by far the best book ever written on Pétain's military career. His other essential work is *Pétain: Général en Chef, 1917–1918,* 2nd ed. (Paris: Presses Universitaires de France, 1997), which provides an in-depth examination of Pétain's command of the French army in the final years of the Great War and highlights his contributions to the Allied victory. Pétain's role in suppressing the French army mutinies of 1917 and his restoration of the French army as a fighting force can be found in Pedroncini's groundbreaking book *Les Mutineries de 1917* (Paris: Presses Universitaires de France, 1967). Unfortunately as of this writing none of Pedroncini's works have been translated into English.

As mentioned earlier, biographies of Pétain that focus on his role as leader of Vichy France dominate the field. Among these, Herbert Lottman's *Pétain: Hero or Traitor?* (New York: Viking, 1985) offers a fair assessment of Pétain's life and especially his activities as head of Vichy. Marc Ferro's *Pétain* (Paris: Fayard, 1987) is a scathing indictment of the marshal, which is typical of the Vichy-focused genre of biographies.

In terms of more general histories with Pétain as a central figure, Robert Doughty's magisterial work *Pyrrhic Victory: French Strategy and Operations in the Great War* (Cambridge, MA: Belknap Press, 2005) provides the definitive account of the French army in World War I. Of particular interest are his insightful portrayals of the major figures of the French high command, including Pétain, in the Great War. Also useful in this regard is Jere Clemens King's *Generals and Politicians: Conflict Between France's High Command, Parliament, and Government, 1914– 1918* (Berkeley: University of California Press, 1951). For World War II and Vichy, Robert Aron's classic book *The Vichy Regime, 1940–1944* (Boston: Beacon Press, 1969) provides a tough but fair assessment of Pétain and Vichy. Robert Paxton's essential work *Vichy France: Old Guard and New Order, 1940–1944* (New York: Columbia University Press, 1972) is a thorough condemnation of Pétain as well as of his regime and its supporters.

Index

Académie française, 83
American Expeditionary Forces (AEF), 58-60, 62-63, 67, 69
Artois, 1, 15, 24-26, 28, 29, 34

British Expeditionary Force (BEF) 1914, 21, 26, 59-61, 68-69
British Expeditionary Force (BEF) 1940, 90-91, 93-94

Castelnau, Edouard-Noel de, 36-37
Champagne, 29-31, 34, 53-54, 63-64
Churchill, Winston, 95-96, 98-99, 102, 107
Clemenceau, Georges, 61-62, 71

Dakar, 99, 102, 103
Daladier, Edouard, 84, 86-87, 89-90, 93, 105, 111
Darlan, Jean-François, 96, 99, 100, 107-108
Darnand, Joseph, 109
D'Esperey, Franchet, 23
Doumergue, Gaston, 84-86
Dreyfus Affair, 6

École de Guerre, 11-12, 14-15
École de Tir, 10-11

Falkenhayn, Erich von, 24-25, 33-35, 40, 47

Foch, Ferdinand, 8, 61-62, 64, 66-67, 69-70, 91, 95, 113, 119
Fort Douaumont, 34, 37-38, 43, 45-46, 48-51, 80, 104, 112
Fort Souville, 43, 50
Fort Vaux, 46, 48, 51, 80
Franco, Francisco, 86-87, 91
Franco-Prussian War, 3-4, 7-9, 18, 22, 34, 71
French Army, 1-7, 11, 14-15, 18-20, 22-24, 28, 29, 31-32, 34-35, 44-45, 49, 53, 55-61, 64, 71-73, 78-79, 82-85, 89-94, 97, 113, 119-120
French Army mutinies (1917), 57-58
French Navy, 96-99, 108

Gamelin, Maurice, 89-91
Gaulle, Charles de, 14-15, 57, 77-78, 86, 95, 102-103, 110-112
Grandmaison, Louis Loizeau de, 8
Guderian, Heinz, 90

Haig, Douglas, 33, 59, 60-61, 68
Herr, Frédéric, 36-38
Hindenburg, Paul von, 47, 60, 68
Hitler, Adolf, ix, 85, 87, 89-90, 94-95, 97, 101, 103-109

Île d'Yeu, ix, 112-113

Joffre, Joseph, 5, 14, 17, 19-20, 22-23, 25-34, 36-37, 44-46, 48, 50, 52-53, 58, 113, 119

Langle de Cary, Ferdinand, 30
Lanrezac, Charles, 18, 20-21
Laval, Pierre, 100, 103-104, 107, 110, 112
Ludendorff, Erich, 47, 51, 60-64
Lyautey, Hubert, 5, 74-75, 84

Maginot Line, 80-83, 86, 90-91, 93
Mangin, Charles, 5, 47-48, 50, 52, 67-68
Marne, First Battle of the (1914), 22-23, 25, 60
Marne, Second Battle of the (1918), 63-68
Mers-el-Kébir, 99, 103
Metz, 69-71
Milice, 109
Moltke, Helmuth von, 19, 24
Montoire, 105-106
Napoleon I, Emperor of the French, 1, 8, 10-11, 71
Napoleon III, Emperor of the French, 1, 3-4
Nivelle, Robert, 45-47, 49, 52-57

offensive à outrance, 7-10, 12, 14, 18-19, 21, 23, 40
Operation Torch, 107

Painlevé, Paul, 54-55, 57, 74

Pershing, John, 58-59, 62, 69
Pétain, Eugénie Hardon, 12, 72, 112-113
Plan XVII, 17-18
Poincaré, Raymond, 17, 48, 55, 71

Reims, 24, 63-66
Resistance, 109
Reynaud, Paul, 90-96, 111
Rif War, 73-77, 87
Rivera, Primo de, 75, 77, 87
Rivières, Raymond Adolphe Séré de, 7, 43
Roosevelt, Franklin, 107
Royal Navy, 98-99

Schlieffen Plan, 19, 82, 90
Second Empire, 1-4
Somme, Battle of (1916), 32-33, 44-46, 48, 51, 53
Sommerville, James, 99-100

Verdun, Battle of (1916), ix, 32-48, 50-54, 69, 77, 79-80, 86, 89, 92, 97, 104, 112-113, 119
Vichy France, ix, 98, 101-104, 106-112, 120-121
Vonderscherr, Colonel, 11

Weygand, Maxime, 91-93, 95-96
Weygand Line, 93-95
Wilhelm II, Kaiser, 24, 33, 47, 70
Wilhelm, Crown Prince of Germany, 35, 42, 46-47, 50, 63, 66, 68,

About the Author

Robert B. Bruce is an associate professor of history at Sam Houston State University where he specializes in European military history with a particular emphasis on World War I, World War II, and the Napoleonic Wars. He is the author of *A Fraternity of Arms: America & France in the Great War*, which won the Tomlinson Prize from the Western Front Association for the best book on World War I and the forthcoming *Verdun: The Battle for France, 1916* which will be published by Harvard University Press. He lives in The Woodlands, Texas.